Health care in
approaches. *Wise*
me, and even mad
embodied here ...conventional,
counterintuitive, an ...all. Read it and find out for
yourself how to think and perform more creatively!

Jack Lewin, MD
Health policy consultant
Washington D.C.

What a brilliant idea—put a winning football coach, a savvy Shakespeare producer, three hard-driving corporate CEOs, a world class dance choreographer and a County Sheriff who deals with jail inmates and SWAT Teams into one room to share best practices, and leadership theories. Common problems and the cross-pollinating creativity and innovation that follows will result in practical lessons for any business.

Jim Volz
Author of *Working in American Theatre* (Methuen Drama)

Wise Beyond Your Field offers a wonderful compilation of the insights of successful leaders in diverse fields and what they have taught each other. All of us suffer from "in the box thinking," but The Gang has broken out of the box to cross-pollinate each other's thoughts on enhancing organizational performance. This is a must-read for any leader attempting to take his or her organization to the next level.

Ted Epperly, MD
CEO, Family Medicine Residency of Idaho
Past President, American Academy of Family Physicians
Author of *Fractured: America's Broken Health Care System and What Must Be Done to Heal It*

We have had the pleasure to support one of The Gang members through our work at the Doris Duke Charitable Foundation, and we believe they epitomize much of The

Gang's approach. Trey McIntyre and Company have, in record time, redefined notions of how and where dance companies can operate, and even what dance companies can do. They are open, entrepreneurial, fearless, imaginative and generous, marrying the worlds of true civic leadership and extraordinary art. The trails they have blazed and the lessons they have learned will be useful, not only for the dance field but also for anyone interested in healthier cultural communities and a healthier, more creative nation.

Ben Cameron
Program Director for the Arts
Doris Duke Charitable Foundation

Wise Beyond your Field offers those who lead and those who seek to lead a journey into innovation and resourcefulness. I recommend the book for leaders who want to challenge themselves and their organizations to be on the cutting edge.

Marilyn Chandler Ford, PhD, CJM
Director, Volusia County Division of Corrections
Daytona Beach, Florida

As traditional civic leadership fractures due to tougher business demands and shorter CEO tenure, communities are in urgent need of new leaders and new leadership coalitions. Watch this one. It may be the model communities are looking for.

Carol Coletta
Director, ArtPlace

Wise Beyond Your Field reinforces my belief that creativity and innovation can make good things happen and play a vital role in progress of human beings anywhere.

Dr. Vuong Quan Hoang
Director, CCI Indochina
Vietnam's Journalism Award Winner 2007
National Book Award Winner 2010

How Creative Leaders
Out Innovate To Out Perform

How Creative Leaders
Out Innovate To Out Perform

Nancy K. Napier and The Gang

The Gang

Jamie Cooper • Mark Hofflund • Don Kemper • Bob Lokken
Chris Petersen • Gary Raney • John Michael Schert

CC!
PRESS
BOISE STATE
UNIVERSITY

PUBLISHED BY CCI PRESS
Boise State University

Managing Editor: Stephanie Chism
Production Manager: Joanna Lui
Cover design by Paul Carew of Carew Co.

ISBN 10: 0-9855305-2-9
ISBN 13: 978-0-9855305-2-5

CCI Press - http://cobe.boisestate.edu/cci/cci-press/
http://cobe.boisestate.edu/cci/wise-beyond-your-field
All trademarks are the property of their respective companies.

To aggressive learners everywhere who do things differently to get better.

TABLE OF CONTENTS

Wise Words

Leaders often express the need for keeping their organizations out of the proverbial rut. Yet, how often do appeals for "out of the box" thinking truly achieve creative innovation?

Wise Beyond Your Field reframes the notion of fresh thinking by exhorting leaders to look beyond themselves and their fields to find truly creative ways of breathing new life into their organizations. Nancy Napier's study of The Gang and their creative approaches to driving success in their organizations—and learning from others—is a revealing look at how today's success isn't always the right formula for tomorrow's triumph.

Chris Petersen's success in building Bronco football into a nationally recognized powerhouse has certainly become a model for what is possible all across our campus at Boise State University, and with the company he keeps in The Gang, his example will always be on the leading edge of the possible.

Concise, simply stated and engaging, Napier's book cements its author's reputation as a leading mind in the dissection and understanding of how creativity and innovation work and how leaders can harness new potential among those they lead.

Dr. Robert Kustra
President, Boise State University

Foreword

Whether you run a business, a nonprofit, a city, a region or a state, innovation is fundamental to sustainable growth. And connectivity is a foundation stone for innovation.

The value of connections in driving innovation is well documented. But to date, most studies of connectivity have focused on the ability of organizations to link their internal "silos" and to build better relationships with their clients and suppliers.

Now, in *Wise Beyond Your Field*, Nancy Napier and The Gang from Boise have exposed the power of a special kind of connection: connecting the odd dots.

Taking on the world, the diverse organizations in The Gang have demonstrated outstanding success in their respective fields of endeavor. That success reflects the ability of The Gang members to build (and strengthen) their organizations by exploring arts, sciences, and experiences which they would not "normally" encounter.

How is it possible to have your own "law enforcement agency of choice"? Why use a blue turf football field? If you tried to sculpt "Relentless Innovation," what would it look like? What happens when you are playing Lady Macbeth and a skunk runs across the stage? *Wise Beyond Your Field* shows how, why, and what, illustrating the power of harnessing "odd connections" to find creative insights and innovative solutions in unexpected places. As this book says, "No diversity, no learning."

For the person who values innovation, *Wise Beyond Your Field* provides a practical approach to moving outside your comfort zone and find great lessons for developing creative leadership capabilities. Napier and her team also demonstrate how to use a "gang" to facilitate that brave move into the unknown.

Once you've read *Wise Beyond Your Field*, you'll be inspired to start connecting your own odd dots.

Of course, for the ever-innovating, there's more to diversity than wildly different backgrounds, different skills and different occupations. There are different continents! So from Boise, Idaho (U.S.), to Brisbane, Queensland (Australia), The Gang's connection of odd dots is globally expanding. There is nothing like going beyond your field than going beyond your continent!

Tony Krimmer
Founder of Odd-Dot Connect Australia and Idea-Lab International
Innovation Facilitator, Innovative Regions Centre
Department of Industry, Innovation, Science, Research and Tertiary Education
Brisbane Technology Park, Brisbane, Australia

Introduction

Mixing Handcuffs, Shoulder Pads, Ballet Shoes, and Laptops

Chris Petersen, Head Football Coach at Boise State University, is not shy when it comes to new challenges. A two-time winner of college football coaching's highest honor, Petersen is a man who has faced down football opponents who were larger and better known, with many times the financial resources of his program. Often he succeeds, much to the surprise of detractors and the delight of fans. Yet, before one event, he felt he was entering a fog, a world so distant from what he normally encountered that he needed help. He turned to his former Special Teams Coach. Originally from Columbus, Ohio, Jeff Choate fills a room with gentle kidding and light-hearted ease—until he starts coaching, and then the room loads up with his intensity. He sports a goatee the color of a burnt-orange autumn leaf, gets kudos from his players as a great special teams coach, and was a high school English teacher in an earlier life. So one day in a staff meeting, when Choate started speaking in iambic pentameter, Petersen knew he had his man.

Petersen and his coaches were planning to attend a meeting later in the day, where he, along with several others in a group he belonged to, would read sections from a speech about a battle in 1453 in France. Reading his part in the St. Crispin's Day Speech, given by King Henry V and written by William Shakespeare, was likely one of the few times that Petersen's heart rate may have gone over its normal level in years. Choate, with his experience in getting distracted teenagers to gain a feel for Shakespeare, brought his magic to the challenge. In the process, he helped Petersen make his acting debut a success and, once again, find creative ideas to help his organization perform better.

But Petersen was not always so convinced.

* * *

"We are not creative here. We're football coaches. We try to do the same thing over and over. It's about routine. I'm just not a creative guy."

Boise State University's Chris Petersen sat across the table from a decidedly non-football person. As a business professor with no sports background, Nancy still confuses wing nut and wingback (and thinks that perhaps a wing back is a chair, rather than a football position). She's baffled by the idea that one position is called a "WEAK side linebacker." That anyone would want to hold a position that says the player is "weak" seems like an open call for serious teasing, especially in a field where men want to be strong, not weak.

So it was just odd for a person so naïve about football to sit across from a football coach, offensive coordinator at the time. This was 2005, and Petersen was having none of the idea that creativity could play a role in what the football program did. Instead, he repeated that to be good, this football program needed structure—in how to train, how to practice, how to recruit, and how to be sure players follow a schedule. As he said, "There's just no room for creativity."

Then again, this is a man whose team plays on a blue field.

Being the cordial gentleman that he is, though, the coach spent the next forty-five minutes of that first talk telling the professor about how the program recruits differently from other teams because it doesn't have the resources or stature of a University of Oklahoma (the Goliath team that Boise State later defeated in a memorable Fiesta Bowl Game in 2007) or University of Oregon (one of his former employers). He talked about how the training is different from that of other teams he's visited or talked to. He mentioned that the hiring of coaches at Boise State focuses on criteria that other programs don't seem to emphasize as much. Nancy came away thinking, "You may SAY you're not creative, but I don't believe it for a moment."

Petersen is not a man to rush into any new-fangled idea or turn of phrase, for that matter. He is thoughtful, takes his time to hear and ponder an idea, and when one comes from out of nowhere, he doesn't immediately invite it into his world. But he became the head coach of the football program later in 2005 and he continued to let the professor come by to chat. It took another year for Petersen to acknowledge that, in fact, the program is different. As he said later, when he looked in the "rearview mirror," he realized that what the program had done for years was not like others.

For another two years, he resisted talking about his program as being "creative," instead preferring the term "innovative." "Creative" sounded too artsy. He's not alone. Most people assume that creativity applies only to theater, dance, music, or film.

But several years later, in an interview with a local newspaper after another bowl game victory, Petersen gave up the fight.

"We like creativity," he said, "we like doing things that others don't."

He now holds his head up and says, "Being creative is just part of who we are."

* * *

Why would a football coach put himself into a situation where he's reading Shakespeare aloud, alongside a software company CEO, a county sheriff, and a world-renowned dancer? As members of The Gang, these high-performing, highly creative leaders model the fundamentals of creativity—going outside of your "comfort zone" to do something that you have never done before (and, may likely never do again!). Petersen did it because he and the others are relentless learners and want their organizations to boost performance beyond what their peers could ever imagine. And much of that demands creative approaches.

The notion of people outside the business world modeling good management or leadership has been around for a very long time. Think of Alexander the Great, Attila the Hun, and General Dwight Eisenhower. But only in the last few decades have we begun seeing more systematic evidence that leaders today are trying to learn from leaders in the past or from leaders in fields far different from their own. Look at the business bestseller lists in the last ten years—they are sprinkled with books that offer wisdom from past military leaders (Sun Tzu, Alexander the Great) and political leaders (Winston Churchill), to sports figures (John Wooden, Phil Jackson) and artists (Twyla Tharp).

Many books focus on creativity—mostly for individuals, some for companies, and a few for countries. Some try to transfer lessons from one field to a very different one; the sports-to-business transfers are likely the most common. But almost none looks at how leaders from several wildly different fields can learn from one another to improve leadership and boost organizational performance. *Wise Beyond Your Field* provides just that, taking an inside look at what leaders in selected high-performing, highly creative organizations across diverse fields have learned—and continue to learn—from each other to push their organizations to ever higher levels of performance. Their lessons can help you and your organization improve as well.

The Gang organizations happen to be based in the most remote and isolated metropolitan area in the United States. Many people would consider Boise, Idaho, to be in the middle of nowhere. It may not be Botswana or Mongolia, but some people might argue it is nearly as isolated. Flying west, from Chicago to Boise the 1,400-mile stretch takes nearly four hours. The Boise region has a population of over 500,000 people, but it is five hours by car to Salt Lake City, and nine hours to Seattle.

So what would organizations and creative leaders based in such an outpost offer leaders in the bigger world? More than might be obvious at first. Finding high performers using creativity in unexpected places may speak to the value of being "out of the way." Fewer resources generally mean that smaller communities and the organizations based there need creativity to stand out nationally or internationally. Also, being in a smaller community may force or encourage interaction among people from very different fields. As one high-tech CEO said, if his firm were in Silicon Valley, he'd spend his time talking to others in the industry. In Boise, where similar firms are rare, he is forced to talk to people outside of his field, which in the end, has become a valuable insight itself. But even if organizations are not in geographically remote sites, it could still be beneficial to find ways to "shrink distances" across disciplines and fields to learn from others.

The Gang started in 2006 with four core members, which became case studies for research on organizational creativity. The group has grown to seven members, each well known within their field for high performance and creativity. By 2010, The Gang organizations included:

- **The Ada County Sheriff's Office**, whose sheriff has taught in Northwestern University's leadership program and is developing new approaches to problems such as inmate housing and communication.

- **The Boise State University Football Program**, which consistently ranks in the top 25 programs nationally, often in the top 10, despite its often much lower level of financial resources than competitor schools.

- **Drake Cooper**, a firm that frequently wins regional and national advertising awards and has built a powerhouse of creative output for a range of clients.

- **Healthwise**, a nonprofit health information provider, that has led the industry in helping people take responsibility for their own health decisions and was named by the *Wall Street Journal* in 2007 as one of the best small businesses to work for.

- **The Idaho Shakespeare Festival**, which has been the focus of a Yale Drama School case study evaluating the theater's unusual business model, which brings unique financial and creative benefits.

- **Trey McIntyre Project**, a renowned contemporary dance company, which spends half the year touring worldwide and receives rave reviews in such publications as *The Washington Post, Le Monde,* and *The New York Times.*

- **WhiteCloud Analytics**, which focuses on helping the U.S. health care industry use its data to dramatically reduce waste and increase the consistency and quality of patient care. Its CEO sold an earlier firm he founded, ProClarity, to the world's largest software company—Microsoft.

Each organization epitomizes the qualities of outstanding creative learning organizations: constant curiosity, non-defensiveness about examining their successes and mistakes, relentless attention to building and preserving strong cultures, and a disciplined approach toward creativity and innovation. The group has gained notoriety and attention in the national media, including *USA Today* and *The Washington Post*, and has done radio interviews and speaking engagements with groups such as the American College of Physician Executives and NASA.

Now it's your chance to learn from these remarkable leaders. We divided the book into two parts. Part I includes eleven Gang Rules that each organization follows. The leaders may have discovered the rules at different times or in different ways, but over the years, each of the organizations has followed these core rules.

The chapters in Part II cover sample ideas, or lessons, from each of the four sectors: law enforcement, football, the arts, and business. Each chapter highlights an idea and shows how others in a different field have used it in their own organizations. For instance, who would expect that the idea of position coaches, so common in football, would find application in business or in dance? Or that the notion of future thinking, so typical for business CEOs, could be novel and valuable in theater or sports? A final chapter provides ideas on how to start your own gang.

Each chapter is short and easy to read, allowing you to start anywhere, dip in and out within a specific field, or read the book from beginning to end. Each chapter also concludes with a "Go Beyond" opportunity to push you to go beyond your current thinking and try to do something different to get better. The "Go Beyond" segments are set off with a "wise head" next to the call to action question or idea.

Finally, a summary of the rules and lessons appears at the end of the book.

We guarantee we will take you out of your field, whatever it may be, and put you squarely into places you never expected to be. You'll find ways to apply ideas that may be routine in one field but out of the blue for yours. And you'll realize that many of the concerns and challenges facing leaders from wildly diverse areas may in fact be more similar than you thought. The examples may seem to come from far afield, but the questions and problems do not. By the end, we hope you too will become wise beyond your field.

Part I

GANG RULES

Part I: GANG RULES

Over the years, Gang members have learned from each other how to boost their organizational success, which we'll cover in more depth in Part II. But leaders of The Gang have also discovered that they have in common eleven basic rules that are fundamental to how they operate and who they are. These rules may play out differently within each organization, but they are critical to what it means for them to be high performers and highly creative organizations. We chose these examples to show how organizations within extremely different sectors can all follow and use them.

1. Rules on Creativity
Rule #1   Look Beyond Your Field
Rule #2   Blend Structure and Creativity
Rule #3   Make Aha! Moments Happen

2. Rules on Attitude
Rule #4   Fear Complacency
Rule #5   Turn Disadvantages into Advantages
Rule #6   Change Your Mind, Not Your Mission

3. Rules on Vision
Rule #7   Think BIG
Rule #8   Build a Culture of Performance
Rule #9   Ask, Don't Tell
Rule #10 Time Your Big Moves
Rule #11 Make the Unimagined Real

1

Rules on Creativity

Rule #1   Look Beyond Your Field

Rule #2   Blend Structure and Creativity

Rule #3   Make Aha! Moments Happen

Rule #1

Look Beyond Your Field

Once best practices are documented within your own field, they become normal practices. So to learn, you have to go outside of your own field. That's what The Gang does for me.

Bob Lokken
CEO, WhiteCloud Analytics

Looking outside a field or discipline for ideas is fundamental to The Gang's success. These organizations, which come from completely different industries, purposes, and ways of operating, have found they can learn from each other and from fields far beyond their own. We'll offer three examples of how Gang members have looked outside their fields or disciplines for creative ways to push for higher performance.

Movies and Software?

Think about the last time you watched a movie at home. How long did you stay with it before deciding to stop and move onto something else? Hollywood has studied just that question, especially given the intense competition for viewer time. Most Americans watch a movie ten to twelve minutes before they decide to continue or stop.

Now think about the last time you thought about buying software, whether new or an upgrade. Your reaction likely reflects what software "user experience" people know. Potential software users are hardhearted compared with movie watchers. How long would you give that software package before choosing whether to buy it? Rather than ten to twelve minutes, a potential software user will devote a mere one to two minutes before deciding if the pain of learning to use the package is worth the benefit. If we watch movies because they grip us emotionally, how could a piece of software "grab the user by the throat" enough in the first two minutes to convince the user that making the effort to learn it will be worth it?

By reaching outside his field, one CEO of a software development firm found a way to fully engage users. The CEO studied the movie industry to understand how to use emotion to pull in viewers and applied it to the software his firm developed. Bob Lokken's firm ProClarity, founded in the late 1990s just as online analytics programs were starting to hit the markets, created software that was far more interesting and user-friendly than anything available then. The software analyzed huge amounts of data and created visuals—clear, easy to understand, and very accessible—that managers could use in making decisions. Not the usual numbers in spreadsheets, the data showed trends and patterns visually, which allowed for easy assessment and decision making. Rather than showing static numbers, the software instead let people "surf" their data, in much the same way they surf the Internet. By reaching outside the software field to study the film world, Lokken found a way to grab potential users emotionally, so they would want to buy and use his product. The firm's market share soared worldwide, so much so that Microsoft bought the company half a dozen years later. The concept of visual representation of massive amounts of data is now commonplace.

Netbooks in Unexpected Places

A father, a mother, and a child want and need to communicate, even when the mother is far away and hard to contact. Experts worry that the mother's location is not a good one for the son to visit, leading perhaps to the son becoming "desensitized" if he saw his mom in that setting. The unit has tried several options for communication among family members, including sending videos and using awkward telephone setups. The most recent arrangement is a Skype-like system, with daily access from 9a.m. until 11p.m. That way, family members and friends can chat more regularly, even when the distances—physical and psychological—may be great.

The mother is not in the military. She's in jail. In a unique arrangement for inmates, the Ada County jail in Idaho was the first in the United States to use what, of course, now seems like an obvious idea: buying $300 netbook computers and using software that is similar to Skype. It saves money, eliminating the $250,000 distance video set ups and the need for glassed walls of telephone booths. It also avoids the potential to desensitize children who visit their mothers or fathers in jail. Experts know that when children visit a relative in jail, they may lose the sense of the jail's being a "bad place" to avoid. The transfer of an idea used widely in business also saves the county $400,000 annually.

Sports in the Arts World

Early in his career with the Idaho Shakespeare Festival Producing Artistic Director Charlie Fee hired a marketing director. She had a background in sports marketing and began to talk about some of the ways that athletic programs and teams "market" themselves. So when Fee commented one day that he was learning about how sports firms sponsored professional athletes, anyone nearby shuddered a bit to think about the possibility of Julius Caesar with a Nike swoosh on his shoulder. While that never came to pass in his organization, the theater does routinely have corporate sponsors for a play or for the run of a season.

While Fee's group does not have sponsorships of individual actors at present, another Gang organization does.

Trey McIntyre Project (TMP) encourages sponsorships of individual dancers in the company. The sponsorships help support the company and the dancer and also create a sense of connection or fan base for the company. TMP's Executive Director, John Michael Schert, like Fee, is taking the concept of sports marketing and pushing it even further. His goal is for the audience members who come to a TMP performance to build the same rabid devotion and "ownership" for the dance company as football or basketball fans have for their favorite teams. Schert's dream is to reach a point where everyone who attends a performance thinks of it as "game day," and comes wearing a TMP T-shirt and other gear. In all cases, these and other Gang members have made looking for new ideas by looking outside their fields part of the habit and routine of creativity.

 Go Beyond: Next time you're in an airport, pick up a magazine you've never read before—*Science* or *People*, or one on gardening or motorcycles. What can you take from it that is different to apply in your organization?

Rule # 2

Blend Structure and Creativity

We need structure, we need order, we need schedules and we need our system taught a certain way. But within that, there needs to be creativity to keep growing, to keep the energy and the enthusiasm. What new wrinkles do we need to make us better?

Chris Petersen
Head Football Coach, Boise State University
USA Today, October 6, 2010

Albert Einstein would understand football coaches and jail deputies, or at least their uniforms. He routinely wore the same (type of) clothes every day, walked the same route, with the same colleagues. Einstein understood the value of routine and structure. With fewer choices to make about the mundane aspects of life, he could focus on more important questions. Routines in some aspects of work and life open up "space" for creative thinking in other areas. Both coaches and jail deputies use this approach to better train players and help people in trouble find ways to reshape their behaviors.

Routine and Structure

During the football season, Boise State coaches wear "uniforms" of khaki trousers and blue or orange football-program-logo shirts just about every day to work, and of course, they wear matching uniforms (shirts or jackets, slacks, hats) for games. When a business manager once asked how the football program could "get ready for a game each week," Coach Chris Petersen's response was, "It takes a year to get ready for a game every week." He meant that the routine the program follows outside of the regular season must be equally as organized as what happens during the fall game season. Practice schedules for the fall, spring and summer are set months in advance. During the season, daily schedules follow a pattern that varies only slightly. The same holds for the off seasons (winter and spring).

Jail deputies likewise wear uniforms, follow and enforce procedures within a dorm, and encourage certain behaviors by inmates. How the deputies open and close locked doors, how they refer to each other and to inmates, or how they move inmates from one location to another depending upon their security levels—all fit within a structured process. Within that structure, though, they generate ideas for new ways to train, build the culture, and perform better every day.

The Gang members also follow fairly common approaches or (structured) processes for creating something new or doing things differently—whether it is an ad campaign, a theater production, or a football game plan. Typically, they review what worked and what has not worked before. Next, they brainstorm for new ideas. Third, they try out ideas/rehearse/practice and decide which ideas to keep and which to toss. Fourth, they beta test/preview/run through the final product or service or play and then they implement by launching the campaign, opening the production, or playing the game. The amount of time for each stage may vary, but the stages themselves are fairly consistent across all of the different organizations.

The Habit of Creative Thinking

One of us recently talked to about sixty businesspeople and government officials in Ketchum, Idaho, near the Sun Valley resort. Like so many small towns, Ketchum was reeling from the economic downturn. The discussion turned to creativity and how it is useful as a routine, everyday habit, not "just during corporate retreats." An elected official in the audience raised her hand.

"But who has time for creativity? The economy is awful. How can you take time to be creative?"

The speaker asked the businesspeople in the room how many were trying to do things differently, to be more creative. Nearly 50 hands went up.

"Now is the perfect time to be creative. If we're not," said one retail shop owner, "we'll die."

Making creativity a habit is a hallmark of The Gang members as well. They know, like the retail shop owner, that using creativity routinely speeds up their ability to solve problems and find ideas, in good times and in bad.

Some organizations build the habit of creativity into meetings. For example, Healthwise, which is an international provider of online health information (it's a content provider for WebMD, among others) is famously "meeting happy." Any time of day, meetings happen—partly to be inclusive and partly to give time for "open thinking" or brainstorming. Over the years, Healthwise leaders have found that about 15% of any meeting's time is routinely devoted to creative idea generation, although some managers are trying to boost that to 25%. This means that in any given meeting, whether it takes an hour, a day or three days, a good proportion of the time is devoted to generating ideas to help solve problems or find new directions.

Although he resisted the idea of creativity when he first heard about it, Head Football Coach Chris Petersen ultimately realized that creativity was useful even in a structured world. Now, he and the other Gang leaders take it for granted: they think in different ways, ask questions and look outside their fields as part of their normal operations. In essence, they've made creativity a habit. Without stopping to think explicitly about it, they simply ask on a regular basis,

"How can we be better, and what can we do differently?" In the process of making creative thinking routine, they also have learned how to encourage and create their own aha! moments.

 Go Beyond: Where do you have structure that you can "use" to allow you more opportunity for creativity? Where can you eliminate structure that inhibits creativity?

Rule #3

Make Aha! Moments Happen

After meeting a few times, I had an epiphany. BAM! I started realizing game-plan wise, there wasn't enough creativity. I started looking at things a different way.

Chris Petersen
Head Football Coach, Boise State University

When Chris Petersen realized that creativity could be of value for his program, he experienced a powerful aha! moment. He's not alone.

Don Kemper, the founder of Healthwise, recalled a critical aha! moment 40 years ago when he heard a speech by the former Assistant Secretary for the U.S. Department of Health, Education and Welfare, Vern Wilson. Wilson's offhand comment that the greatest untapped resource in health care was the patient hit Kemper's aha! button. In that instant, Kemper grasped that individuals could, and should, take control over and make decisions about their own health, rather than relinquishing that responsibility to professionals. That idea became the cornerstone of his organization's mission—helping people make better health decisions.

Likewise, software CEO Bob Lokken remembered exactly where he was when he recognized the Internet's value in terms of its intuitive way of operating. During the early stages of the Internet's growth, he asked a group of about 40 people how many of them had ever had training in how to use an Internet browser. Not one hand went up. Then he asked how many had ever had training on how to use a new piece of software, whether Microsoft Word or

Excel, or a data analysis package. About two-thirds of the hands went up.

Why, Lokken asked himself, do we need no training for the Internet but we do need it for software programs? Why not make software programs as intuitive as the Internet had become for users? That was the seed for his business-intelligence analytics firm's visually based ProClarity package.

* * *

An aha! moment is sudden awareness—of understanding something or of a solution to a problem. Teenagers who realize the world does not revolve solely around them, middle-aged businesspeople who decide that more money may not be the answer to happiness, the leader who finds a way to build a sustainable culture...all can experience sudden insight.

But rather than being unpredictable, always sudden and generating complete clarity, aha! moments can be the opposite. Many Gang leaders have learned that aha! moments follow a process that can be encouraged, may happen suddenly, or may emerge slowly.

Somewhat like using structure to help encourage creativity, the process of reaching aha! moments generally follows three broad stages. Some people go through the phases faster than others or they may return to an earlier stage, but the process seems to hold across different types of people and organizations. Generally, the three stages include sorting information, sparking the insight, and then confirming or checking to see if it holds up over time and scrutiny.

The sort phase means collecting and sifting through lots of incoming information to learn about a topic or solve a problem. The information could be dumped upon a person, like football players trying to understand new plays. It could be self-sought information, as when an engineer is trying to learn a new job. Regardless, people try to gain some sense of understanding of a question, an issue, or a problem, but typically feel overwhelmed by the speed and quantity of information. Sometimes an aha! moment emerges in this phase, often not.

After sorting comes a "spark" phase. Because it requires more right-brain thinking, many people bypass it or try to rush through, and fail to generate new insights. The techniques encompass, for example, evaluating a problem from a very different perspective, drawing on ideas outside one's field, or looking for what might be missing.

Lastly, once an aha! moment happens, it becomes valuable only when a person can validate or check it, take it to a broader level that will allow for use and learning beyond that particular moment. People test the idea on colleagues who are experts within their fields and check it against people who are not experts. As one of Einstein's colleagues once suggested, "Make it simple enough that a barmaid can understand it." If both experts and "barmaids" understand the idea, it gains more credibility.

When Aha! Moments Don't Happen

During the course of working together over the years, several Gang leaders would comment that they didn't have those dramatic BAM! epiphanies as much as they did earlier in their careers. Why? As they talked through their current situations, we discovered that they had increasingly incorporated the spark techniques into their general thinking. Rather than explicitly stopping to ask, "How can I think about this in another way," or ask, "What am I missing," they do it as a matter of course. It has become routine to look at a problem from multiple perspectives, to think in reverse, to put odd ideas together, and to mull and take a break and have the confidence that a solution or understanding will come. Like the discipline of creativity, they have made generating aha! moments a matter of course.

Go Beyond: Next time you have an aha! moment, dissect it: Did you go through the sort, spark, and check phases? Try to do so when you "need" insight the next time. Then build in the spark techniques to speed the process.

2

Rules on Attitude

Rule #4

Fear Complacency

During the economic slump, someone in our organization said, "We're not changing fast enough." We can never let that happen again.

Jamie Cooper
CEO, Drake Cooper

On June 18, 2005, Harlan Hale changed the course of an organization. He didn't start a Ponzi scheme, buy a company, or become an elected official. That day, two jail deputies escorted Hale—the most dangerous of about 1,000 inmates in the Ada County jail—outside for an hour of sunshine on a brilliant, blue-sky day. When it was time for him to return to his solitary-confinement cell, Hale got lucky. The deputies left two doors open (against regulations), unlocked Hale's belly chains and leg chains before he entered his cell (against regulations), and succumbed to a sly trick when Hale reached for a mop to "clean up the floor a bit," as was his jail job. Instead, Hale escaped. He raced through the unlocked doors, broke a hasp on a locked chain-link-fence gate that deputies had never thought could be broken, crawled up and onto the roof, jumped fences with razor wire, and disappeared for 10 days. He was caught 400 miles away, after obtaining a gun, stealing a car, and running from the police. Hale is serving a life sentence, but will be eligible for parole in 2030.

Harlan Hale has the earnest look of an insurance salesman, save for the 18" long tattoo of a black bat that stretches across his clavicle, almost shoulder to shoulder. Before his escape, he had been arrested for the attempted murder of a police officer and had led police on a long chase. Hale had also been a meth user. But, as the deputies who know him tell it, he's also cunning and smart when he's sober, and on that June day he used his wits and shocked the employees of what had been one of the country's safest jails. Rarely had an Ada County inmate been hurt, killed, or committed suicide and never had such a dangerous inmate escaped.

The security breaches (open doors, removal of belly and leg chains) were embarrassing and inexcusable mistakes. As the Ada County sheriff admitted, if any had not occurred, the escape would not have happened. As a result, a few deputies were let go, the jail updated its security procedures, and most people thought the problem was resolved. But Ada County Sheriff Gary Raney disagreed and eventually had an aha! moment about the event. One day a few months later, he said, "The escape was the worst thing…and the *best* thing that could ever happen to the jail."

Never Waste a Good Crisis

Raney prefers to "never waste a good crisis" and he certainly used this one well. Prior to the escape, the jail had run smoothly for 20 years, so employees believed they were doing a good job. But Raney saw the escape—and his newness in the sheriff's job—as a chance to do a thorough review of the jail and its operations. He studied information about the facility, the employees, and the operations. He asked his subordinates for feedback and he hired an external consultant to conduct an evaluation. At some point during the process, Raney had an aha! moment where he realized that the situation was not just about security issues. He saw a much deeper and more fundamental problem, which he called "the cancer of complacency." That insight helped him realize that the organization needed to change.

Over the next 18 months, the nearly 300 jail employees went through a gut-wrenching process of rethinking the unit's purpose, and eventually reached a "collective aha!" They came up with three "pillars" that drive every decision and action by each jail employee: the safety of staff, the security of the facility, and the well-being of inmates. The process also sparked a change in mindset to one of seeking constant improvement, finding ways to do things better (and differently), and never, ever becoming complacent again.

Desperately Fearing Complacency

In the marketing and advertising firm Drake Cooper, the CEO Jamie Cooper discovered complacency another way. During the economic downturn, one of his employees said, "We're not changing fast enough to keep up with what's happening around us." To avoid falling behind, Cooper and his colleagues had to change fast to adapt to a new environment. Part of their new normal involves constant learning. To spark this, for example, the firm asks two employees each month to design and facilitate a learning experience that is fun, meaningful, and something others can use right away.

The shift in mindset from (possible) complacency to always improving is what each Gang organization now strives for. Members desperately fear becoming complacent, and that translates into looking for ways to improve every day.

While many organizations might look to competitors for ideas on ways to improve, these organizations rarely do. If they do look to other organizations within their fields, as sometimes happens within the Boise State football program, they seek to learn from others who are not direct competitors (or not yet, at any rate). Some, like the nonprofit Idaho Shakespeare Festival, find that financial concerns keep them always "hungry," forcing organizational members to constantly seek ways to improve themselves. As cuts in budgets meant cutting one full-time position, for example, two employees decided to reorganize the tasks from their positions plus the lost full time slot and found new ways to manage the work.

Whatever the trigger for doing so, Gang members constantly look for ways to improve their organizations, regardless of how their peers may do things. As one CEO said, "We're looking for ways to improve that others in the industry haven't even thought about."

Go Beyond: Ask yourself today, "Where can we do things differently to get better?" Find three places.

Rule #5

Turn Disadvantages into Advantages

I have had all of the disadvantages required for success.

Larry Ellison
CEO, Oracle

Gang members have chips on their shoulders—and they are proud of it. They thrive on stories about how living in a remote city or being a small and unknown organization forced them to turn disadvantages into advantages. The David and Goliath stories of Boise State University's football team competing against much larger and better-funded programs have forced it to become smarter and more nimble. Other Gang organizations often encounter equally daunting challengers in their own fields. ProClarity, the business-intelligence analytics software firm that Bob Lokken built before selling it to Microsoft, is a classic example of creatively turning what most people would see as a significant disadvantage into an advantage.

Competing Against Giants

"David" ProClarity, with 150 employees, faced "Goliath" software competitors in its early days of online business analytics. The tiny unknown firm faced the dual challenge of entering a newly emerging market (online analytics) and finding its own niche in that market. In the late 1990s, potential customers had little idea of what "online analytics" could do, let alone how to choose among competing firms. So the obvious decision, if they bought this new type of product, was to go to a well-known firm, like Microsoft, that could provide safe offerings, as well as the training and support they would need.

That was ProClarity's dilemma: its resources (people, money, and time) were nothing compared to established giants. By throwing millions of dollars into the development and marketing of any product, Microsoft consistently overwhelmed smaller firms like ProClarity that were trying to establish themselves in the new market space. Microsoft could offer thousands of potential customers a chance to try out a product for free. Those users were then likely to ask their corporate purchasers to buy that product rather than another they hadn't tried out. Or, Microsoft could go directly to corporate buyers with its worldwide marketing staff. In contrast, ProClarity's CEO, Bob Lokken, felt that, in some ways, *he* was the marketing staff, visiting potential and current customers. However, as one person, he couldn't compete with Microsoft, as well as with many other competitors. So he found a way to turn the disadvantage of being a smaller, "resource-less" firm into one that found an untapped advantage.

Lokken is a man who can't talk without drawing. He has a notebook or whiteboard in arm's length wherever he is. So to explain how ProClarity turned its disadvantage of size into an advantage, he drew three concentric circles on a whiteboard. The outer circle represented potential users of any piece of software—a huge, diverse marketplace of people worldwide. This is where Microsoft and others could put millions of marketing dollars and smother any other entrant into a market. The middle circle, for Lokken, represented software purchasers within those potential user companies. Again, larger firms like Microsoft often targeted the purchasers who made the final decisions on which software packages to buy. Once again, that group was large, and a small firm like ProClarity simply lacked the money and staff to visit those purchasers in a systematic way.

But Lokken saw something others missed: a way to get around the might of Microsoft and larger competitors. He tapped his black marker on the whiteboard, pointing to the innermost circle, and said, "Those are the 'thought leaders' in an industry. That's the group we had to win over, not the potential users, not the buyers. That's where the little guy could have an impact."

These thought leaders were relatively untouched by direct marketing, and instead responded to more personal efforts. They wrote for trade journals and magazines about upcoming products. They also acted as "guinea pigs," beta testing new products, and thus could influence potential users' choices to try and buy new products. That was the advantage that ProClarity used, focusing limited resources in a guerilla manner. ProClarity went after the industry thought leaders in a deeper, more focused manner. With this smaller audience of thought leaders, ProClarity could match and even exceed the resources of competitors, even with fewer people. That was certainly not the case with the huge potential user market.

Finally, ProClarity's products were quite different from what was on the market at the time, because they were visually based and interactive, and thus much easier to use than more traditional analytics methods, which were spreadsheet-based. The idea itself was new and difficult to sell to potential users before they "saw" it. The thought leaders were more open to new ideas and products and offered a way for ProClarity to paint a picture of the new software and leverage its marketing capability, thus turning a disadvantage into an advantage for the firm. If the thought leaders liked the product, they could in essence help introduce and sell the idea of this new type of software for ProClarity. And, indeed they did and ProClarity took off.

Surprises of Isolation

Other examples of turning a perceived (by others) disadvantage into an advantage happen within many of The Gang members, such as the dance group that located far away from acknowledged arts centers and has been able to create a market for its performances as it helps shape the community. Healthwise uses the organization's remote location as a way to disarm big-name potential customers, from New York to London. The organization's address—Bogus Basin Road—makes it sound questionable but allows the executives to surprise clients with their competence. "They have to visit to see if we are real," CEO Don Kemper notes "and once they do, we always win them over."

Go Beyond: What do you think your three biggest disadvantages are? Turn at least one around and make it an advantage.

Rule #6

Change Your Mind, Not Your Mission

> *Remember that to change thy mind and to follow him that sets thee right, is to be none the less the free agent that thou wast before.*

Marcus Aurelius (121-180)
Meditations. viii. 16.

We mentioned in the Introduction that Chris Petersen took a while before he was convinced of the value of creativity for his program. As he says, it was an epiphany and he's been a strong advocate ever since. So what changed his mind?

In late 2005, Petersen moved to the Head Football Coach's office, which, during the off-season, looks onto the (in)famous bright blue football field that startled many fans flipping through ESPN football games before the program made a name for itself. That field has given many people in the university a license, if not an obligation, to "try something new."

Now, when someone brings up a wild idea, others are conditioned to say, "Why not? We've got that blue field out there giving us the right to try." The blue turf, the professor, and listening to others who watched the program helped Petersen realize that creativity was indeed a part of what he did, even if he didn't want to admit it at first.

In addition, Petersen reads—a lot. He reads business books and magazines, like *Good to Great* and the *Harvard Business Review*. In fact, in his very organized office next to the field, a leather sofa and two comfortable chairs surround a coffee table covered with current and back issues of the magazine. Even his assistant, Vicki Sullivan, has said, "That's all we read around here." Boise State's football players may have been on the cover of *Sports Illustrated*, but for Petersen, what really matters is what he can learn from sources beyond football. Some of his recent reading materials include books on Apple's Steve Jobs, *The Corner Office* interviews with CEOs, and even Marcus Aurelius.

Ultimately, Petersen's willingness to be open to ideas that sounded wacky to him initially, or that seemed to have no relevance, paid off for him and his fellow Gang members. Now, when Nancy tosses out new and strange ideas, he cocks his head and squints, trying to figure out whether the idea has merit, but he's open to listening. As he said in an early Gang meeting, "I never know what she's going to ask me or talk about, but I always learn something when we meet." And as Marcus Aurelius so wisely said nearly 2000 years ago, changing your mind doesn't mean changing your mission or who you are.

What Others Change Their Minds About

Fifteen years ago, Sheriff Gary Raney was a "cop's cop." He wanted to write tickets, "get the bad guys" and put them away for a long time. But at some point, he stopped and asked a bigger question: What's the purpose of patrol and the jail? What outcomes are we really seeking? As a result, he realized that "writing tickets" (for revenue mostly) was not the real goal of law enforcement. Instead, it's a question of how to make communities safer. That shift in mindset to outcomes (rather than process, which writing tickets is) means that he looks for ways to "make a difference" in the safety of the community. That has, to some degree, resulted in patrol officers writing *fewer* tickets. Instead, they solve problems and educate. In other words, rather than immediately writing a ticket, they stop people and talk about why speeding makes the community less safe or why having a burned-out taillight or iced windows can be dangerous for the driver who doesn't see a bicyclist as easily. Outcomes, not processes, mean that any decision a person in the agency makes has to contribute to achieving the organizational goals. Raney changed his mind, clarified the mission and helped boost the organization's performance in the process.

Go Beyond: When's the last time you changed your mind about something important? Why or why haven't you considered changing?

3

Rules on Vision

Rule #7

Think BIG

You have to think big to be big.

Claude M. Bristol (1891-1951)
Lawyer, lecturer, investment banker,
foreign correspondent, and writer

How could a tiny software firm capture the leader's share of the world's emerging market in its field of online analytics? How could a health information provider headquartered on a street called "Bogus Basin" entice people to trust its information in over one billion user sessions? How does a young dance company with ten dancers and a choreographer build a reputation that brings invitations and commissions from around the world and has become one of four U.S. cultural ambassador organizations? How does a football program that has a total program budget that is less than the salaries of many of its opponents' head coaches manage to succeed? How do they do it? They all think BIG.

The Gang members are relatively small organizations— the largest being the Ada County Sheriff's Office, with 600 people. The others range in size from 25 to 220 people. Yet, in each case, the organizations have excelled in their fields, in large part because the leaders were able to set goals and visions that were bigger than what any of their peers could have imagined would be possible.

At Healthwise, one "think big" breakthrough came from calculating that over 300 million major health decisions are made annually in the United States alone. According to CEO Don Kemper, that realization helped spur employees to recognize that when decisions were made without

Healthwise information, the decision maker was at a big disadvantage. The result: a quantum leap in the scope of solutions that evolved out of the organization.

For the Trey McIntyre Project (TMP) dance group, thinking big came partly because the two founders had prior exposure to the dance scene nationally and internationally, one as a choreographer and the other as a dancer. They knew what and how other groups performed. They knew that Trey McIntyre's choreography was unlike others anywhere and they knew that people who saw performances were ready for more. But a big leap was moving from the artistic vision to an organizational one. TMP's leaders and members began to think like firms known for strong brands and culture, high quality, and vision. The group believes it is doing something major that is worthy of worldwide recognition and everything it does supports that.

Once that foundation was set, the group explicitly sought out and accepted invitations in dance venues and locations worldwide that would add to their visibility and reputation, ranging from many cities in Europe and Latin America to small and large cities in the United States.   On a local level, once the group chose Boise as a home base, it aggressively became part of the community, making inroads in many ways. For example, the dancers performed numerous "SpUrbans," or spontaneous urban dances, done on the spot in downtown locations. Dancers mingled among the crowds, then suddenly burst out and danced for one to two minutes, then blended back into the crowd. The group performed at hospitals and corporations, in schools and clubs. The group also pursued and received numerous grants, donations, and support from within the community and from beyond. It became the city's first economic development cultural ambassador and was a U.S. cultural ambassador, visiting four countries in Asia as part of the DanceMotion USA program of the U.S. Department of State and Brooklyn Academy of Music (BAM). For TMP, the vision was, and is, to be known globally but also to help shape the local community. In four years, according to the local and national press, it is succeeding in doing just that.

Go Beyond: What is one BIG thing you'd like your organization to do? What would it take to get there?

Rule #8

Build a Culture of Performance

You know what really keeps me up at night? Hiring the right people, finding who will fit our organization. People with high output and low egos. OKGs—our kinda guys.

Chris Petersen
Head Football Coach, Boise State University

Finding people who will fit into an organization is a major part of any leader's job, and that holds for The Gang as well. The football program, for example, seeks what the coaches call OKGs—our kinda guys—code for students and coaches who have integrity and humility but are also competitive. They look for people who want to get better and get things done: in other words, "high output, low egos." The veteran football players have recognized those qualities and what makes the program different on and off the field. They use several words consistently: "It's like a family; coaches and players look out for you." But even more fundamentally, they mention "accountability and competing in everything you do...against yourself in the classroom to improve, and on the field to be the best you can be."

When it comes to recruiting players, the football program has a clearly biased approach: They look for OKGs and do so deliberately. As the coaches say, "We look for great kids and good football players." The technical skills are something to improve; it's the character and personality, or as Petersen says, the "intangibles," that the coaches investigate deeply. As the program has improved in quality and rankings, more young players seek out Boise State, which means that the coaches have more sifting to do, but they've learned to keep looking for the right people to keep the culture strong.

* * *

Don Kemper founded Healthwise over 35 years ago, and while its product and service lines have changed, its purpose and mission have not: it is a nonprofit international provider of online, by-phone, and in-print health information and tools "that help people make better health decisions." For example, content for the trusted WebMD site comes out of Healthwise. Today Healthwise is known nearly as much for its work culture as it is for its effectiveness and reach of consumer health information.

However, the Healthwise culture took time to develop. Kemper's first boss was a professional engineer who ruled with an iron hand and a grim smile, and so early on, Kemper had a poster in his Healthwise office of a huge orangutan with the caption, "When I want your opinion, I'll beat it out of you." At some point, he realized that people weren't laughing. So he set about changing the atmosphere.

What came next was a long, sustained effort to build a culture that reflected the core values of respect, teamwork, and always doing the right thing. For the next two decades, Healthwise stayed small enough for Kemper to know everyone, allowing him to be the face and soul of the organization's culture. As the organization grew, it was harder to maintain Kemper's direct ties, but the culture has remained a high priority. A telling illustration is the Healthwise employee satisfaction survey. Conducted every six months, the survey has a 95% participation rate and is 100% anonymous. Employees score the organization as a whole, their teams, and their cross-team work. They even rate their sense of the respect and freedom to speak their minds.

Healthwise executives read every handwritten comment, good and bad. All comments, with a few edits to protect the principle of respect, are available to the entire staff, after which the executive team holds a fireside chat to respond to issues or questions raised. During the chats, each executive responsible for an area with negative feedback responds to the comments publicly, explaining what the organization will do, if action is possible, or why something is unable to change. Again, the process helps reinforce respect, teamwork, and doing the right thing, the principles of the Healthwise culture. Any question or issue is open for discussion. Employees may not always agree with decisions, but they certainly will know why managers make them.

Bigger Than Ourselves

Like the football program and Healthwise, Gang members repeatedly talk about the importance of culture as an aspect of competitive advantage that is critical for success. Trey McIntyre Project people talk about finding their own version of OKGs: "people we like and want to be around" and who want to do something that is "bigger than themselves" and help their community. The Ada County Sheriff's Office now typically attracts 100 applicants for most jobs, as criminology students and law enforcement officers have heard about the agency as a "great place to work." All of Drake Cooper's employees participated in making the firm's "crest" that includes fundamental elements critical for the organization: Share it (spread ideas), Plus it (make something original and make everything you do better), Say it (be honest, be open), and Love it (work hard but make time for the rest of life). WhiteCloud's CEO, Bob Lokken, like Chris Petersen, focuses on "high output, low ego" in the culture, or as he puts it: "It's not who is right but doing what is right."

Make It Happen

So what do these organizations do to create these cultures? First, they take charge of developing and implementing the culture they want. As Boise State's Chris Petersen says, "You will have a culture no matter what you do—you can build the culture or it can develop around you. Your choice." So each of these top leaders has crafted, usually with others, key components of the cultures in terms of the attitudes, behaviors, and relationships to expect, model, and nurture.

Next, the leaders recognize that they are key in implementing and enforcing culture. They are insistent that the leader "be in the trenches" to model and talk (frequently) about the culture. As Healthwise's CEO, Don Kemper, says, "You have to focus on it every minute. Otherwise, it can slip away."

Third, Gang leaders have learned that a sustained strong culture comes by "promoting it through the middle," similar to the ways they encourage ideas throughout their organizations. Even if the leader can develop and try to model the culture, it needs more critical mass than one or a few leaders. Sheriff Gary Raney works with key sergeants to help them understand the vision and culture for the organization and then relies heavily on them to help carry it forward. Football coaches look to the veteran, older players and encourage them to help instill in the younger players the behaviors, attitudes, and relationships that reflect the culture.

Last, these leaders know that culture and high performance don't come from one or a few things. Interestingly, many people query The Gang leaders, asking, "What do you do to get people to act that way?" Hoping for a simple, easy response, outsiders may look at the visible elements or even some idiosyncratic aspects that reflect culture. Healthwise allows (behaved) dogs in the workplace, Drake Cooper has a generous flextime program, ProClarity had beer in a refrigerator and a Ping-Pong table, and the football program has a blue field. Yet The Gang members know that it's not a single aspect or a few aspects that "make" a culture. It's many visible and invisible elements; but more important, it is the integration of these elements, which is much harder to do and to describe. In fact, one coach commented years ago that he didn't mind if others wanted to "look at our program because, even if the others pick up a few ideas, it's the complete and constant integration—pulling together—of the pieces that make it unique."

As Healthwise's CEO, Don Kemper, puts it, "An advantage of a simple mission statement is that it allows everything you do to be tied to a single concept." At Healthwise, as is true with other Gang members, the mission and the culture are deeply intertwined. The culture is strengthened by the mission of helping people make better health decisions. The mission is strengthened by the culture: respect, teamwork, and doing the right thing. When people believe in a common purpose and feel they belong to a common culture, coming to work each day becomes more of a passion than an obligation.

 Go Beyond: What "kinda guys" do you hire and why? How do they contribute—or detract—from the culture you want for your organization?

Rule #9

Ask, Don't Tell

As leaders, probably the most important role we can play is asking the right questions.

Tim Brown
CEO, IDEO

Starting tomorrow, pay attention to the questions you ask (or that you do not ask) in a normal day. When do you ask questions? For what purposes? How do questions help you learn? Do they help you connect or engage with others? Do you use questions to solve a problem? Or, do questions help you anticipate or find problems you want to avoid?

The Gang leaders are masters at asking, not telling, yet they know that not all questions are equal and that questions have many different purposes. We'll cover at least four uses: to understand, to engage and build trust, to solve, and to find or anticipate problems.

Questions to Understand

A former attorney for the Ada County Sheriff's Office often joined review meetings where senior managers and investigating officers wrestled with controversial cases. The discussion covered what had happened and the implications, and, if necessary, recommendations on how to better handle future situations. During the meetings, detectives or patrol officers typically described a scene, the actions they and others took, and their rationale. The lawyer, as the one person outside the enforcement ranks, usually did not know the case, understand the jargon, or see the situation as the law enforcement officers had.

But she could do something that came as naturally to the detectives and patrol officers as it did to her: she slowed things down and asked questions. Law enforcement officers, jail deputies, and detectives are good at "slowing things down," especially when it comes to defusing dangerous situations.

The attorney also slowed the discussion and asked questions that may have seemed naïve to the experts in the room. She might ask a detective to repeat exactly what he found or the reasons for his actions, and to do so in simple language. As he spoke, it sometimes became obvious that he may not have seen or understood as clearly as he had initially thought.

The attorney used her role as the non-expert to "play stupid." By asking naïve questions and insisting that explanations be jargon-free, she achieved two goals. First, she understood the situation better, which could help her deal with any legal action, but, equally important, she also helped the experts see the situation differently and perhaps reach new solutions or conclusions.

Questions to Connect, Engage and Build Trust

Steven Covey's book *The Speed of Trust* argues that when people trust each other, productive work can happen faster. Rather than needing to stop often to explain reasoning or terms, people who trust one another agree that—at least in some situations—they will act because a colleague says it's important to do so, without requiring a long explanation. Building trust, though, takes time and often demands questions from one to another so each person can know the other and understand the other's thinking and motives. Used this way—to connect with people, engage them, and learn to trust each other—questions build an understanding of other people, which in turn leads to implicit communication.

Coaches use questions with each other and, even more so, with their players. To engage young men, many of whom have short attention spans, to connect with them, and to build trust among players and between players and coaches, the coaches often use questions during team meetings. Also, questions allow coaches to see just how much a player understands about his role and position and how he fits into the "broader concept" or scheme of a game plan and of the program. In the process, trust grows among coaches and players, speeding the process of becoming a unit.

Questions to Solve Problems

Following the escape of the Ada County Jail's most dangerous inmate, Sheriff Gary Raney and his second-in-command, Major Ron Freeman, used questions to identify what the agency could do to go from being "good enough" to being great. The two questions posed to jail employees seemed simple, but as one employee said, "They shook us to the core."

- Why does this jail exist?
- What are the three most important things we should be doing here?

Over time, with much discussion, the employees came up with three "pillars" or core values that everyone could remember and use in any decision, every day: safety of the staff, security of the facility, and well-being of the inmates. They were clear, simple and easy to remember. And they have become fully incorporated into daily decisions made by every jail employee.

Questions to Find Problems

Finally, Gang members have learned to use questions to anticipate problems or to identify areas for improvement. Some members have made these sorts of questions routine practice. Aaron Shepherd, a lieutenant at the Ada County jail, asks every new employee to look consciously for what is "different" and to ask questions about it. When new employees join his unit, he "requires" them to constantly question and ask why they or the unit do things certain ways. Before employees become too accustomed to how this jail works, he wants them to look at all processes and systems with fresh eyes and ask, "Why do you do it this way?" as a method to come up with improvements.

Another organization's leader deliberately asks questions of himself and his leaders. Healthwise's executive team focuses on "skating to where we think the puck will be." In health care, the puck often seems deflected—with new government policies, medical discoveries, or technical breakthroughs. So when new information comes out of these three areas, the organization's executives ask themselves, "How does this change our thinking? How does it change our plan?" With every subtle change in the rules or in the interpretation of the rules, the creative leader re-asks the basic questions, yet again.

Go Beyond: Try asking at least 10 questions today before lunch. What's the reaction?

Rule #10

Time Your Big Moves

The early bird gets the worm, but the second mouse gets the cheese.

Willie Nelson
Country music singer

Boise State University's Head Football Coach Chris Petersen may not say much, but his eyes are always on the move. They jump, shift, and then zero in on a target, whether a football play, one of his players, or an idea. In addition to watching, though, he also listens to an inner gut, a voice from years of experience that can tell him when something feels right or off-kilter. As that small voice gets louder, he tucks his observation on a shelf, from where he can pull it out now and then, check whether he still thinks and feels that his observations are right, and look for more insights into what might be happening and why.

During the fall of 2009, Petersen thought he saw a problem, even when others did not. Game after game, the team returned with victories. By the fourth week of the season, though, practice seemed just a little "off" to him. During the fourth game, Petersen's eyes and gut confirmed that something wasn't quite right—execution wasn't "on." He continued to keep his thoughts to himself, though, even as Boise State University roared through another game. Apparently, others didn't notice (yet), since the coaches, players, and reporters were all pleased and confident at the way the season was going. But by the end of the next week of practice, however, Petersen's instincts told him things were not right: energy was down, players were just going through the motions, and focus was drifting. The next game, against the University of California, Davis, was a win, but as he and the other coaches and even some players said, "It felt like a loss."

The team struggled during the game. Players lacked the zip that fans expect from this underdog program gone "big time." By the time that game took place, other coaches had also seen that something wasn't quite right. Petersen, who had been mulling the "something" for several weeks before the others noticed it, brought the coaches together on a Sunday afternoon, the day after the game.

Good coaches are expert technicians in their areas, but they are also good teachers who put in long days during the season as well as during the "off-season." During the fall semester, the weekly schedule is intense and full. During the week, they often go from 6:30 a.m. until 9 p.m., Monday through Wednesday. Thursdays are "date nights," so everyone knocks off about 6 p.m., but otherwise, the coaches spend lots of time with one another thinking about and planning for the upcoming game. Each day is planned in detail (long before the season begins) in terms of what the focus during practice will be, what the goals are, and how they develop the game plan and carry out practice.

On Sundays, coaches review videotapes from the previous day's game, identify what plays worked well, and choose certain areas to focus on for improvement in the coming week. The Sunday following the UC Davis game, however, Petersen and his coaches spent an hour talking about the "something" that had been nagging him: What was going on and, why things seemed "off." As Associate Head Coach/Offensive Line Coach Chris Strausser said, "For guys in football to talk so much is amazing. For us to spend a whole hour, on a Sunday, in the middle of tape review, to talk about this, was even more unusual." As they talked through what seemed to be happening (or not happening), they agreed "something wasn't right." So they took a step back and, made a significant mid-course correction, even though the "rest of the world" didn't see that anything was wrong. After all, the team was winning.

Then Petersen talked to the players. He spoke in a way that made the players think they were the ones who had identified the problem: lack of energy, lack of focus, and making mistakes that they shouldn't. By the end of the session, the players and coaches agreed that going "back to the fundamentals" was critical. They needed to make sure everything they did—in the training room, in practice, on the field—was done with deliberate and concentrated focus on improvement. The players came away thinking the mid-course correction had been their idea, and as a result, they were even more committed to make the changes.

How did Petersen "know" that something was not working but even more important, how did he decide when "the time was right" to make a change? When do coaches know when to make a move, to change something, whether on the field or in the training room? What does it take to gain the intuition and the confidence to read a situation and know when to act—or when not to act? For Petersen, much of this comes back to an ability to observe and see what is not moving solidly toward improvement to get better.

Think Forward for Future Implementation

For others, timing can relate to the introduction of a product or service. Being ahead of the market is a pain—but it's much better than lagging. In 2000, Don Kemper of Healthwise had an aha! moment: The Internet was not enough for delivering Healthwise's content. Even though users could "pull" free information from the Internet through hundreds of websites, most people still made health decisions in relative ignorance. To reach more people and influence more decisions, Healthwise developed a "push" strategy as well.

By 2002, Kemper and Molly Mettler, Senior Vice-President for mission, co-authored *Information Therapy,* a book about "Ix," or the prescription of the right information to the right person at the right time as part of the delivery of care. Health care leaders understood and embraced the Ix concept, but little changed for many years. The technology and policies were not in place and the content was not quite right for the push approach. So instead, Healthwise created the Center for Information Therapy, which eventually became an independent nonprofit organization in Washington D.C. that continued to "push" the Ix idea. A decade later, information therapy is now a requirement for federal reimbursements to doctors for the cost of their electronic medical record systems.

 Go Beyond: When did you last use timing to make a change and why? How can you use it better?

Rule #11

Make the Unimagined Real

If you can dream it, you can do it.
Attributed to Walt Disney

Great leaders have visions that may be invisible or simply unimaginable to those around them. Their strength is in making that vision real, something tangible, even when it's not. It happens in the theater, on the football field, and in business. One Gang leader did just that when he helped a group of people imagine and then turn into reality the idea of an outdoor experience that could happen "indoors."

In the theater world, most people are familiar with the notion of a "black box." Once lights go down, the dark theater is like a box with one lighted side where the action takes place. For those who have experienced only that formal setting, trying to imagine anything else can be challenging. Charlie Fee, Producing Artistic Director for Great Lakes Theater (Cleveland, Ohio) had a vision to do just that when he asked his Cleveland-based board members to find a way to renovate a theater to bring an outdoor theater experience indoors.

The board members' idea of a "real" theater was the 1920s Art Deco Ohio Theatre in downtown Cleveland, with 1,200 seats, a large stage, and big velvet curtains, as any reputable theater should offer. When Fee talked about an "outdoor theater experience that was indoors," they had no clue what he meant. So he began a campaign—to help them visualize an experience, not a place, that they had never heard of before.

Fee was also managing at the Idaho Shakespeare Festival in Idaho. That theater, a 600-seat amphitheater, is open to the sky, which is clear and starry for nearly all of the 80 plus nights of summer productions. In contrast to the half-filled Ohio theater, 90% of seats at the outdoor theater are full all season long, meaning that more than 50,000 people come every year. Hearing that the Idaho theater filled up nearly every night, compared with the Cleveland theater's 50% full house record, the Ohio contingent was ready to listen.

The Idaho experience offers plays for everyone, from kids to 80+ year olds, with seating options that meet different budgets and physical abilities, from "sitting on the ground" lawn seats, to boxes of tables seating from four to six people, to seats higher in the stands, to blankets on the berm. Fee or Managing Director Mark Hofflund bound on stage before performances to welcome and thank patrons and supporters. They often ask for input for the next season and warn guests about the neighborhood skunk that has been wandering across the stage.

Visitors bring picnic dinners and wine and get up to use the restrooms or go for more wine, even during the play itself (although they watch for sword carrying soldiers rushing down the aisles). Conveying this "experience" to people in Ohio meant Fee had to show some of it but in an old-fashioned setting, and then build from there. He started with "curtain talks" so familiar in Idaho but unheard of in more formal Ohio. When Fee first walked onto the lighted stage and stood in front of the heavy curtains to welcome patrons, explain a little about the play, and thank sponsors, the audience was stunned and a bit uncomfortable. But he saw it as step one toward making the unimagined real.

Next, Fee sought to change a decision by the board that "no wine" could be taken inside the theater. Whereas Idaho patrons brought their own wine, drank it throughout the production, and often went for more at intermission, the Ohio crowd had to gulp a plastic glass during the 10-minute intermission and race back inside. When the board agreed to try this unorthodox change, the Ohio audience loved it.

Finally, Fee gave the board and staff members from Ohio a real sense of the "experience." They visited the outdoor site in Idaho to feel first-hand the informality and of the interaction between audience, actors, and setting, especially when something "went wrong." In an outdoor setting, the weather, the skunks, and the geese flying overhead may all contribute to unexpected outcomes or, simply, mistakes. To see how the actors and the audience dealt with them, always with humor, also contributed to the experience that Fee wanted to recreate indoors.

By helping people see what they could not imagine, Fee was able to generate interest and commitment to the renovation of the Hanna Theater in Cleveland, to create something unique in the world of indoor theaters. The theater has seven different seating options, from the traditional to balcony boxes, from banquettes and loose club chairs to the "ultimate freedom" lounge and bar seating, where you can watch the production and order wine. In addition, the theater is much more audience-friendly than traditional ones. It allows patrons not only to go behind the scenes before the show and meet the cast afterward but also to visit the theater for a variety of other activities: Salon Thursdays, Happy Hour Fridays, Nightcap Saturdays, and, as is common in Idaho, Director's Night, a preshow discussion before the first night of all productions   How do leaders make the unimagined or invisible real to others? They start by having a vision themselves and then finding ways to make it become tangible to others, as other Gang members do as well.

"Make It Mine"

In the software world, making the imagined real is also tough. To do this, Bob Lokken, as CEO at ProClarity, developed an extensive software-visualization tool kit to mock up solutions, a process that would engage users and help them see the solution. The company also built functional prototypes using the customers' own data, since nothing is as powerful as "seeing your own data." A customer could, in essence, "make it mine." While other firms demonstrated solutions with fictitious numbers, ProClarity created sample visualizations from customers' actual data. The result: potential users could see what did not exist and imagine themselves using the product and their own information. The solution became theirs.

A last example of making the unimagined real comes from an experience that Healthwise's CEO, Don Kemper, had a decade ago. When he first saw a video game show called "You Don't Know Jack," Kemper was put off. Jack, the game show host, was an obnoxious big mouth who seemed to watch over your shoulder as you played the game. Jack's comments on guesses or even pauses irritated and then intrigued Kemper. What if, instead of an obnoxious game host, Jack became an empathetic and knowledgeable health coach; guiding people through a learning experience about their health problem and helping them create an action plan?

Healthwise later licensed Jack's development software from its creator, Jellyvision, and built a coach called Shelly, with a warm and understanding voice. In over 15 interactive "conversations," Shelly uses motivational interviewing and cognitive behavioral therapy to coach people through key learning and plan-setting activities.

While users loved the conversations, Healthwise clients didn't know how to value a virtual coach like Shelly and too often categorized the conversations as "interactive videos." While technically accurate, the designation downplays the power of the experience. So Healthwise repackaged the virtual coach in terms of "visits," which individual users—and now clients—value. Now positioned as "Shelly Visits," the experience is another way of making the unimagined real for those who have not yet experienced it.

Go Beyond: What is something that few can imagine doing in your organization? "Make it real" for them.

Part II

GANG LESSONS

Part II: GANG LESSONS

While Gang members may be similar in the rules they follow, they are, at bottom, in quite different sectors and environments. Over the years, they have learned that activities or practices that they use and assume are common may not be in other sectors. Their relentless curiosity and openness to looking beyond their own fields is the core of how they have learned from each other. This next part of the book, then, is where we see the wisdom they've gained from one another—and how applicable the lessons are far outside an industry or sector.

Part II has four sections, each one providing some lessons from a given sector that the others have begun to use in their own organizations. We will see lessons from law enforcement, football, the stage, and business. As you read, check how your organization might adapt some of what may seem like far-fetched ideas from beyond your field.

4. Lessons From the Jail and Patrol
Lesson #1   Use Reverse Thinking
Lesson #2   See What's Missing
Lesson #3   Seek Ideas From All Levels
Lesson #4   Build a Problem-Solving Mindset

5. Lessons From the (Blue) Turf
Lesson #5   Use Whole-Part-Whole-Learning
Lesson #6   Get Better EDD (Every Damn Day)
Lesson #7   Develop Position Coaches
Lesson #8   Be Urgent in Practice, Calm in Games

6. Lessons From the Stage
Lesson #9   Practice to Improvise
Lesson #10   Build Unexpected Partnerships
Lesson #11   Create New Business Models

7. Lessons From the Boardroom

4

Lessons From the Jail and Patrol

Lesson #1

Use Reverse Thinking

I've always liked the minds of criminals, they seem similar to artists.

Richard Linklater
Film director and screen writer

Sergeant Gary Grunewald brought the deputies on his shift together one night to ask them to think in reverse. He didn't know he was doing that, and they certainly didn't, but he set in motion a new way of thinking that has infiltrated the Ada County jail.

Deputies in the jail receive regular training—about procedures and policies, about how to interact with and show respect for inmates while maintaining control in the dorms, about how to watch for potential fights or inmates who don't get along, and about topics like how inmates might try to escape or create weapons. But rarely do they escape or make weapons themselves.

Sgt. Grunewald changed that for a week. His 32 jail deputies worked four, 12-hour shifts. The deputies worked in the dorms of 92 inmates or in other areas of the jail facility—transferring inmates to and from meeting rooms, to the courthouse for trial, to medical facilities – or in other security functions. Grunewald decided to give the day-shift deputies a challenge: a contest during the coming week's shift to create the most lethal weapon and a rope that would hold the weight of a person during an escape. Each deputy received the same items that an inmate receives when she or he is booked into the jail. In addition to an orange jump suit, an inmate receives a white plastic grocery bag that contains:

- A cup and spoon
- A toothbrush and toothpaste
- Bedding and a towel
- Jail clothes and underwear

Grunewald told the deputies that by the end of the week's shift, the deputies who came up with the "best" stabbing weapon, striking weapon and rope would win the contest. The sheriff and the major would judge the resulting weapons. Also, as is common during the regular shift, deputies were tested on policies and procedures within the jail to be sure they were up to date with their knowledge. Those who performed particularly well on the test would receive an additional "potential weapon item"—such as a comb—something that might be available to some of the inmates.

After the contest, Major Ron Freeman dumped the deputy-made weapons onto a conference table. Ropes made from braided plastic bags and strips from the orange jumpsuit and knives made from toothbrush handles or combs were among the most common weapons. But the winning weapon was a three-inch long knife, short enough to fit in the palm of a small man or woman. To test how lethal it was, the head of the medical staff "attacked" a pumpkin. (This was during the week of Halloween.) The handle was made from a toothbrush whittled down to be two inches long. Orange clothing strips were wrapped around the handle for a better grip. The knife won the contest because of how lethal the sharpened toothbrush was and because its size was concealable, small enough to be used almost without being seen.

Deputies often receive training on how inmates might create weapons, but the contest was the first time that deputies were asked to "think in reverse," or to think like inmates. Rather than speculate about what inmates might do or create as weapons, they "became" inmates and shaped weapons. Reverse thinking now is common practice for deputies who want to anticipate what might happen in their shifts.

What Do Other Organizations Do?

Other organizations use variations of thinking in reverse in many ways. The small business analytics software firm's attempt to try and influence the smaller group of thought leaders, rather than the more typical potential user group or Trey McIntyre Project's decision to move to a remote outpost rather than to a larger city exemplify cases where thinking in reverse can lead to an advantage. In the first case, the software CEO realized he could not compete with the power of larger firms in getting potential users to consider buying his product. So instead of going directly against those competitors, he found a different group to approach: the thought leaders, smaller and influential but at that time not tapped as a resource for software firms. By thinking in a way opposite to what people in the industry were doing, he circumvented the normal practice to find one that worked better for his firm.

In the case of the dance company Trey McIntyre Project, the decision to base the group in a remote location was viewed with shock and now admiration by others in the arts world. For that group, in particular, it has created a new business model because it took a reverse, opposite approach—by not moving to the acknowledged (and assumed) arts "centers" of the country or world, but rather to an isolated site.

Go Beyond: What is a big problem you're facing? Try turning your solutions "upside down" and see if you get new ideas.

Lesson #2

See What's Missing

And now here is my secret, a very simple secret; it is only with the heart that one can see rightly, what is essential is invisible to the eye.

Antoine de Saint-Exupery (1900-1944)
Author

Lieutenant Aaron Shepherd has a square face with a triangle point chin. He tends to look downward at times, making his conversation partner think he's shy or maybe not listening. But like other well-trained law enforcement officers, Shepherd sees and hears more in an hour than many people may see or hear in a week. He is one of the jail's top leaders, managing the jail's staff of both commissioned officers, who carry weapons, and noncommissioned staff who support the operations. He is the type of person who asks new staff members to question everything they see during the first month on the job, because he trusts their fresh eyes to see and wonder about "the way things are done" much more than people who have gotten used to the operations or who have become complacent.

Several years ago, Shepherd faced a vexing contradiction with two jail shifts—one during the day, one at night. Each shift had about 27 commissioned deputies, working 12-hour days, four days a week. The teams traded night and day shifts regularly. At a shift's end, each team reported what incidents had occurred in the dorms, such as whether inmates had fought or smuggled in weapons or other contraband. In his review of statistics on a regular basis, Shepherd saw a disturbing pattern: consistently, one team reported significantly more "action" than the other. Shepherd noticed that the quantity and nature of the incidents within the same dorm could be quite different between the day and night shifts. Why would one team be able to keep the dorm "quiet" while the other had many more incidents? Also, and more puzzling, the night shift was the one reporting more incidents, which did not make sense intuitively, since the inmates should be less active at night.

Any reasonable analysis would lead to the conclusion that one team kept the inmates under control and the other was causing some of the incidents by creating some of the disturbance, or as Shepherd said, "Stirring things up." Another idea was that one team was simply unable to keep inmate behavior in line or unable to manage them.

But then Shepherd looked for what he might be missing. With more investigation, he realized that the quiet, no-action team might in fact be too laid-back, too relaxed about following procedures and enforcing policy about what happened in the dorm. In essence, the no action team was being complacent, while the other team was finding and solving problems in the dorms, as it should be.

This ability to see what's missing or what's not there is a sense that some jail deputies and detectives alike develop over time. One deputy has said that jail deputies have to be able to "see" even when it may seem that nothing is happening. Sometimes, a dorm may be too quiet, which can signal that the inmates are planning something or that they are keeping something from the deputy and don't want him or her to know what's happening. This ability to sense when things seem too quiet, which could mean potential danger was what Shepherd discovered. The team with the action was better at anticipating or sensing when something might be wrong and pursued it, which often led to reporting of incidents in the cellblocks. The other team, whose shifts all remained quiet, was not finding out about some of the incidents, and thus reported fewer.

Since Shepherd went below the initial or surface level findings of the statistics to understand what might be missing and what else he could ferret out, he uncovered a situation that he remedied diplomatically with the supervisor of the team that had not seen as much action. In this case, by understanding the implications of what was not there, Shepherd helped his subordinates begin to see their role in a larger way, a key element of insight thinking.

Missing "Movement"

In addition to using the movie industry to create software that was emotionally appealing, Bob Lokken of ProClarity recognized and then applied another insight to his software. An advantage of the Internet, in addition to being intuitive and thus requiring no training for most people, is that people can navigate or move around in ways that are not linear. A user can move forward, "sideways" (by taking a detour and looking up something interesting that crops up unexpectedly), or backward. In other words, part of what Lokken realized about the Internet's use is that it mimics the way our brains work: We don't always move in a forward, linear fashion, we often skip around, we go back, forward, and sideways, and we stop and start over. He built those features into the business analytics software the firm developed: going forward, going backward, and changing areas of focus in the middle of the analysis. By seeing what others in the software world did not see (at the time), he was able to create a valuable niche.

 Go Beyond: Look at trends on the edges of your industry. What can you see that others might miss? How can you take advantage of them?

Lesson #3

Seek Ideas From All Levels

The ideas I stand for are not mine. I borrowed them from Socrates. I swiped them from Chesterfield. I stole them from Jesus. And I put them in a book. If you don't like their Rules, whose would you use?

Dale Carnegie (1888-1955)
Author of *How to Win Friends and Influence People* (1936)

Jail Sergeant Justin Ryan grew up with a stepfather and a biological father who were not around much when he was a child. By age 11, Ryan was, in his words, "raising himself." By his own admission, he got into trouble before finding that he needed structure, which athletics in high school provided, and he ultimately learned that he could do anything he set his mind to. His tough upbringing might suggest that being a maverick is second nature for him, and it is, but not as he might have expected when he was younger. It turns out he's a driving creative force in making the Ada County jail a better organization.

Upon promotion to sergeant, overseeing 32 jail deputies, Ryan wanted very much to learn how to perform well in his new job. He asked more senior people, for instance, how to choose a lead or a key back-up person for each team when the sergeant was away. While veteran sergeants tended to choose the same one or two leads from their teams, Ryan chose unexpected leads and rotated the position among his deputies. His approach became a good training device and spread knowledge and a sense of responsibility throughout his team. Small move, big impact. Other sergeants have since imitated the practice in their own teams.

Perhaps emboldened by his initial success, Ryan next tried a development process he called "The Legacy Wheel." The wheel helps deputies identify characteristics that make for top-notch officers, depending upon the specific job they hold. For example, Ryan asked deputies to identify the characteristics of a good detention officer and to decide, on a one-to-ten scale, which characteristics made such an officer a "10." Next, he asked his deputies to rank themselves on the same scale (one to ten) on those characteristics, and he used their responses to help the deputies build development plans to improve. The process worked in large part because Ryan asked deputies to create their own lists of what makes a good officer, rather than imposing existing ones on them. Interestingly, the characteristics that emerged were similar to what Ryan would have included but, given the deputies' chance to identify them, they felt a greater sense of ownership.

By chance, another sergeant heard about Ryan's Legacy Wheel. She modified it for her own use. When she brought together her 28 deputies and divided them into four groups, she asked each group to choose the strongest leader within the group. Next, she brought those four people to the front of the room and then queried each team on why that person had been chosen as a leader. In many cases, the chosen person was shocked, having had no idea that others thought of him or her as a leader. As the group discussed what characteristics the selected leaders had in common, attitude came up repeatedly: She helps out, is positive, and looks out for other people. The deputies saw the value of the exercise, the importance of attitude, and the importance of having peers evaluate each other.

Both sergeants took the initiative to prototype an idea. In a sense, the exercises became an example of ideas coming from all levels in an organization: One sergeant tried an idea, another saw and modified it, and others have since taken and improved on both. In doing so, they exemplified the agency's culture of avoiding complacency and trying new ideas that would help to boost overall performance.

Relentless Innovation

Sometimes artifacts and symbols can reinforce critical ideas and goals. "Relentless innovation" is one of Healthwise's key organizational competencies, and each employee knows it just walking into the building. A 20-foot Lyman Whitaker wind sculpture—named "Relentless Innovation"—stands near the entrance to the corporate office. The base is solid and grounded, but the upper part moves as the environment changes, like the organization wants its employees and products to be: Grounded in the mission but responding to the environment. In addition, the sculpture reminds anyone entering the building that innovation needs to be relentless and is the responsibility of all within the organization.

Football Training That's Fun

Tim Socha is Boise State University's Strength Training Coach for all sports, and he's learned something from Chris Petersen that is similar to what goes on in the jail: ideas need to come from all levels, not just from the top. When Chris Petersen asked Socha to prepare a training program before a bowl game several years ago, Socha was shocked at Petersen's response to what he had prepared.

"Nope. This won't work. I want you to come up with a training program that achieves the goals we have—get them fitter, stronger, faster—but uses NOTHING you've ever done before in training. And, it's got to be fun."

As Socha tells the story, his initial reaction included a few "choice words" back in his office, but then he began to see what Petersen was driving at—find a way to achieve key outcomes using new approaches that were fun and would make the players better. And he did it. From that point on, Socha began to look for and develop new approaches to training—perhaps small tweaks to what he had done in the past, but he developed them, without being asked.

Socha now says that he asks for and gets good ideas from his assistants in all sports disciplines. Even more interesting, he and other coaches, like Defensive Coach Bob Gregory, say that the athletes themselves are coming up with ideas—for training, for plays, and for ways to build the program, all of which shows the power of ideas from all levels.

 Go Beyond: Today, try to find a new idea from people in at least three different areas or levels of your organization.

Lesson #4

Build a Problem-Solving Mindset

We can't solve problems by using the same kind of thinking we used when we created them.

Albert Einstein (1879-1955)
Physicist and philosopher

My greatest challenge has been to change the mindset of people. Mindsets play strange tricks on us. We see things the way our minds have instructed our eyes to see.

Muhammad Yunus
Founder of Grameen Bank

One spring Saturday night, a patrol officer for the Ada County Sheriff's Office stopped two teenagers who were racing their cars along a highway near their upscale suburban homes. The officer ticketed each of the boys, sent them home, and told them to talk to their parents about it. Normally, the story of law enforcement would end there. But this one doesn't.

On Sunday afternoon, the officer visited each boy's home to talk with the parents and their sons about the incident. He chatted for a while with each family, listening to the parents and sons talk about what happened, how the parents were dealing with what the boys had done, in terms of punishment, and future expectations. The officer asked each of the boys to bring him the ticket he had written. And then, the patrol officer ripped them in half.

The officer's decision resulted largely from his problem-solving mindset, increasingly a core of the agency's expectation and empowerment of employees. That visit to each home allowed the officer to evaluate how he felt the families were dealing with the incident, which he decided was reasonable and appropriate. In that process, the officer shifted from "enforcing the law" to "education" about the law. His two actions—going to visit each family and voiding the tickets—made a greater impact than if he had simply done what would normally be expected for his job, to give a ticket for breaking a law.

The story has become a symbol of how Sheriff Gary Raney and the agency want to be perceived by the public, as "the law enforcement agency of choice," and by employees as a good place to work, where they are empowered and accountable for solving problems, even when that means tearing up tickets. In fact, Sergeant Pat Calley, who supervises patrol officers, says he encourages them to "patrol with purpose," which typically means enhancing safety education in whatever ways they can. He has commented that it's not the "number of tickets we write but the safety education we do."

That means officers must evaluate whether using an incident as a way to teach a young person about why it's important not to speed or race on a highway will have greater long-term safety impact. The patrol officer who stopped the teenagers was closer to that situation than others in the agency and he had the authority to make a judgment on what to do. When he saw how the families responded, his decision was that he could have more long-term impact—for the teenagers' learning about safety and perhaps avoiding potential future traffic violations—by invalidating the ticket.

The "patrol officer who tore up the ticket" story made its way to other law enforcement agencies in the region and prompted a leader of one of the other agencies to call Raney and ask, "What do you do over there to get people to act like that?"

Raney said that the Sheriff's Office was trying to help instill a "problem-solving mindset" in the organization, at all levels in all jobs. But it is quite a different way of thinking—as the officer story illustrated. It means solving a problem, not just "enforcing the law."

The rationale makes good sense. Patrol officers cannot be everywhere to "enforce," but when they have opportunities to "educate," that may well spread the word better (because it is unexpected and unusual) than a teenager reporting that he got a ticket over the weekend.

Problem-Solving Mindset, Problem-Solving Fit

Coach Chris Petersen admitted a few years ago that he was frustrated with the problems that came to his door. But then he had a mini-aha! moment. When he realized that dealing with problems wasn't something that "got in the way of doing my job, it *is* my job," his mind shifted to looking for ways to anticipate and find problems. He's since pushed that mindset to his coaches and players. But even further, and similar to the Sheriff's Office, sometimes intense situations demand that staff be able to dispatch problems quickly and efficiently. When hiring new coaches, in particular, Petersen looks for whether there will be problem-solving "fit."

In hiring coaches, he assumes that anyone at the level where his program plays has the football technical knowledge, has worked with players successfully, and has been in a few other programs. During a recent hiring process, he commented on the number of highly qualified candidates, from NFL coaches to head coaches from other university programs. But his decision to hire rested largely on whether a new coach would have the same problem-solving "fit" that his current ones did. He and other Gang leaders find that problem-solving fit is critical, especially among top managers. As many say, "We think alike but not the same," meaning they hold similar cultural values but have different ways to look at a problem.

Go Beyond: Do you need to shift your thinking—from process to outcomes—in any area of your organization?

5

Lessons From the (Blue) Turf

Lesson #5

Use Whole-Part-Whole Learning

Learning is not attained by chance. It must be sought for with ardor and attended to with diligence.

Abigail Adams (1744-1818)
Wife and mother of U.S. presidents

Several years ago, Boise State University's Head Football Coach Chris Petersen commented that his players come to the university for four (or five) years and that some need two and a half years to "get it." By that, he meant the full range of both obvious and less obvious aspects the students need to understand. From the standpoint of the football program itself, he wanted them to understand the program's "system" in the approach to training, practice, and games. He also wanted them to understand how to be successful college students on top of being athletes. The program's culture includes core values of accountability, honesty, and integrity, as well as the complete focus and deliberateness that a player should bring to practice every day. As part of the process, each year the students set goals for the team, relating to football (such as winning a bowl game) but also relating to academics. One year, the goal was for 55 players to have grade point averages of 3.0 or better. Petersen was proud to report that the team had one of the highest overall GPA's of any of the athletic teams in the university.

Over the years, the coaches have developed some techniques to help their student players "get it faster." One approach is "whole-part-whole" learning. Common among sports coaches, whole-part-whole learning starts by overwhelming new players with information about the program, the values and culture, along with the roles they play (the "whole"). Players say that the amount and speed of information coming at them makes them feel they are standing in front of a fire hose. Even players who enter the program thinking they are well versed in the game feel swamped with the flood of information, since Petersen's approach includes far more than "football smarts" to include the organization's values and system or culture as well.

Next, within each position (e.g., defensive lineman, running back, or wide receiver), the coaches work with small groups of players on the "parts" they need to learn—where to align, where to place their feet, or what position to hold their heads in. The regular team meetings, which are about 30 minutes long twice daily, focus on building player knowledge and understanding the plays along with their specific positions and actions.

Then, Petersen returns to give them more of the whole, the larger picture of how they fit into the team, the program, the university, and the community. Being sure that players understand the system and values of the program is so important for Petersen and his coaches that they require weekly written tests of the players on various aspects of the program. Then it's back to the parts when position coaches meet with players daily on their specific tasks and positions.

The constant shift in perspectives (whole to part to whole to part) builds players' understanding of the program's system and bigger picture, at least for most of them, but it also subtly encourages other critical abilities that are important regardless of what careers they pursue beyond college athletics. By shifting repeatedly from big picture to details, students become better at understanding the program's goals and how the units and parts fit together.

In addition, the constant variation in perspective helps players become more flexible and comfortable with unrelenting change, which is important in most any job.

How Do Other Gang Members Use Football's Whole-Part-Whole Learning Approach?

When Chris Petersen explained his approach to the other Gang CEOs, they needed just a few minutes to grasp the idea and think of ways to apply it within their own organizations. Sheriff Gary Raney's agency is the only governmental entity in The Gang, and he immediately saw the benefits. Part of his challenge is to be sure that employees avoid complacency, stay vibrant, and never become too satisfied with the way the organization runs. Whole-part-whole learning provides more sense of the whole to his employees on a regular basis.

The Sheriff's Office gives new employees an orientation when they start their jobs. That orientation includes the big picture—the history and objectives of the entire organization—before employees go deep into the details and parts of their new positions. But other than that introductory big picture orientation, management does not revisit the broader picture with most employees. Some may get a larger sense because of the jobs they do—for example, being involved in a special project or working on strategic planning. But most rarely receive information on the whole picture on any regular basis. After hearing about Petersen's approach, Raney's agency began to hold regular meetings with employees to provide a state of the organization beyond their units.

Likewise, CEO Bob Lokken could see application even in his latest start-up venture, WhiteCloud. Growing his firm from 2 to 20 people in a year before even introducing a product onto the market, Lokken wants employees to understand the goals of the firm, and then to get into their own jobs and move forward. But he realizes that with any start-up the pressure and urgency is intense. So he now wants to build in cycles of pulling employees back up a level or two so they can see the big picture more frequently, particularly in a health care environment that is changing daily.

Finally, in addition to helping employees keep the larger picture of an organization in mind, the method also instills a flexibility of thinking—shifting perspectives from the detail to the broader view, which for some also encourages reaching outside of a single discipline or field.

Go Beyond: Where could you build in the shift from big picture to details to big picture in your organization?

Lesson #6

Get Better EDD (Every Damn Day)

I hear and I forget. I see and I remember. I do and I understand.

Confucius (551-479 BC)

Confucius had it right over 2500 years ago. Humans learn better when they bring in more of their senses and when they can experience a concept, not just hear about it or talk about it. In football and other physical activities, players hear and talk about a play, watch it on film, and do it on the practice field. And then, they do it all over again. The four laws of learning—explain, demonstrate, imitate, and repeat—match Confucius' ideas of hear, see, do (and then do again). For football players, that means seeing, hearing, feeling (the hit), even smelling or tasting (sweat). In addition, players may learn about and practice a given play four, six, or eight times, depending upon its complexity.

Chris Petersen has been an athlete and coach for 25 years. As a coach with a master's degree in education, he's worked particularly hard trying to find new and better ways to prepare his players for games, especially during practice sessions. With NCAA regulations increasingly setting standards and limits on how many hours and when players would be allowed to practice, Petersen knew that programs that stayed on the leading curve would need to find ways to do it better, more effectively. When he began reading Geoff Colvin's *Talent is Overrated,* he discovered there's more to practice than he'd thought. As Petersen says, "You take what you've got and find ways to make it better."

Petersen's football program does not "fire" players. Once they are recruited, assuming they do what they are asked, and don't get into major trouble, the coaches start with the raw material the players bring and try to make it better. He's finding that deliberate practice for all players is one way that improvement happens every day, or as the Nike slogan on the back of Boise State players' T-shirts says, "EDD" (Every Damn Day).

Practice is fundamental in music, acting, dance, sports, and in anything where the body has to perform at a high level. So what could be new? As Petersen learned, deliberate, purposeful practice can make a good player into a great player, but only when certain conditions exist and are understood: (1) the goal of deliberate practice is to improve; (2) lots of repetitions are critical; (3) always give feedback; (4) practice must be mentally demanding, meaning that if it's done right, two hours a day may be enough; (5) self-observation and self-evaluation become part of the way to improve; and (6) deliberate practice is "hard."

All of this may sound somewhat familiar to anyone who has tried to learn piano or clarinet, ballet or tennis. Plenty of fields use deliberate practice to improve. From surgery to the arts to sports to SWAT team officers—all demand some physical muscle memory and, with purposeful practice, could improve.

So when it comes to this kind of deliberate practice, sports (and dance and acting and police work) may have a real advantage over business. When Bob Lokken, the CEO of WhiteCloud, first heard about purposeful practice, he made connections within his own firm's situation and started thinking about how it might apply to a business setting. At first, he was stumped—software and intellectual-property-based firms don't "practice" as a performing artist or an athlete would, or could they?

Lokken realized that his firm had a "disconnect" between bringing in the smartest and best people managers could find and then letting a Darwinian model take over: survival of the fittest. Those who excel rise to the top. The rest are cleared out and a new pool of recruits comes in. Not only is that expensive, but it defies the logic applied to finding the best people possible. That led him to think about how to use purposeful practice as a way to develop people in a business setting where intellectual property is critical.

From the notion of finding ways to practice deliberately came two outcomes. First, Lokken applied practice to preparation of presentations and interaction with clients. Salespeople would practice, get feedback, focus on specific areas for improvement, and repeat. This is not a new idea, but it generated an attitude of consistent improvement, not just preparation for the meeting at hand. The focus shifted beyond preparation and outcome, to include emphasis on critical feedback on execution, lessons learned, and constant improvement and learning.

Second, Lokken initiated the idea of "position coaches" throughout the company. In the firm, a "coach" develops areas for purposeful practice and improvement that requires repetition. Development, continuous improvement, and continual learning are now ingrained in the organization, part of its DNA. No longer are these critical factors left solely to individual prerogative or happenstance. Execution, review, learning, and improvement happen every day, every week, and in every person's job, so that "participation and engagement are not optional."

A final example comes from an organization that is still working on how to take the simple idea of getting better "every damn day" and execute it in an office setting. When Healthwise's Don Kemper heard Chris Petersen say that "getting better EDD" is his focus, rather than winning, it was a revelation. Healthwise constantly seeks the next idea in consumer health and ways to get it to clients as quickly as possible. But what about "getting better every day"? Clearly, products get better every day but what about people? Could

Kemper get better as a CEO, today? Could his executive team be better today than they were yesterday? Could the writing, the technology, the quality assurance get better? And what would that look like? As Kemper says now, getting better every day is an idea that Healthwise will focus on, EDD.

Go Beyond: Where can you use deliberate practice to get better EDD in your organization?

Lesson #7

Develop Position Coaches

Excellence is an art won by training and habituation. We do not act rightly because we have virtue or excellence, but we rather have those because we have acted rightly. We are what we repeatedly do. Excellence, then, is not an act but a habit.

Aristotle (384-322 BC)
Philosopher

For a non-football person, watching football coaches talk through game plans seems a bit like what it must be for a non-music person observing a composer create a bar of music. There is a calm fluidity of seeking and creating the "right" patterns and fitting perfect notes together: shuffling plays in and out of the possible ones to use, looking at what sounds and looks right at any given point, removing and adding, and giving the plays names that charm the ear or tug at a smile, like "Tiger, move to far RT FIRE" or "Cluster, Deuce Right Hoof."

The coaches sit in the dark, watching film of the day's practice over and over, from a variety of camera positions. Each person in the room looks for something specific and may observe moves and aspects of a play that others might not; sometimes a coach comments out loud about a move or a mistake. Mostly, they sit without talking, watching four to five seconds of a play; then they rewatch it, over and over. Once in a while, a coach will recall a play from an earlier game and ask for that film to come up. In one case, a coach asked to see a play from a game in 2002, "about 50 plays into the game." That he could recall a particular play nearly a decade before is striking to an outsider. Granted, though, like any other sport, business or theatrical production, there are moments that anyone who's an expert will remember. Still, the pure amount of information can seem overwhelming to outsiders, and even players feel it. One former player, who pursued a master's degree in accounting, commented that when he first began training as a freshman, the information came at him so fast and so furiously, he felt he was trying to learn Chinese in a week.

By the end of the week before a game, the coaches and players will have a game plan that could have as many as 70-85 possible offensive and 40-50 defensive plays, several of which are options or extras, but many of which they will likely use. In a 12-14 game season, the number of plays that coaches and offensive and defensive players need to learn can rise to the hundreds, including tweaks and variations during the season. Lots of information, lots of physical moves, and lots of variables to learn to be able to execute flawlessly.

For the approximately 10 different positions in football, each coach works with 4-18 players in a specific position, and some oversee more than one position (e.g., special teams and tight ends). They work with players to help them reach the point where the "fundamentals" are ingrained and the players can act without having to think explicitly about what to do. Football players learn by hearing, seeing, and doing, and then doing again and again. But they really understand when their bodies feel and remember the moves, which comes through repeated practice. Only later might they have an aha! moment when they understand *why* something feels right.

The role of position coaches, then, in football is fundamental to the way the program works. A good position coach helps players understand the "big and the small": the way that a particular position fits into the whole scheme of a play and a team, as well as the details of that position. Finally, once players have those physical and eventually mental fundamentals, the coach tries to build excellence in each player for a given position. In some cases, when the players themselves become quite good at a position, they can help train younger players as well, taking a bit of the coaching role themselves. And this is when a player starts to "take off," when he can teach it to others.

Position Coaches in Business

So how could the idea of position coaches work beyond the sports world? Bob Lokken, CEO of software firm WhiteCloud, is attempting to do just that. His firm now has five "position coaches" around certain topics or areas of the company, including engineering, consulting, marketing/sales, and leadership.

The senior managers and the "best" in the area agree on what the fundamentals are within each position and then fit them to organizational goals. For example, the team identified nine characteristics of great software source code, such as writing "enough" but not over-writing or over-engineering. Then the position coaches developed, with other experts, a training process for engineers to learn and practice those nine characteristics.

Next, the software position coaches go through four steps with engineers, similar to what position coaches in football do: Explain it, demonstrate it, imitate it and practice it. They explain and then demonstrate what good or "elegant" code looks like. Additionally, the coach leads engineers through code practice and reviews, has them imitate what she or he has learned, and then they demonstrate the concepts. For example, coaches may stress that reducing the amount of code can be a "good" thing because it reduces the chances that something can go wrong, which over time could increase the cost and burden of maintenance. Finally, the engineering team continually practices, repeats, and refines the principles, while simultaneously writing more code and getting the product to market.

The software firm is tweaking the idea of position coaches, as it should, since learning across different disciplines means finding ways to apply and use an idea that best fits the new situation. Thus, one difference from the football position coach system is that the WhiteCloud position coach roles will rotate. So within a specific area, over time, each "team member" will become the position coach. It may be somewhat like the older football players helping younger ones, but the software firm's intention to rotate position coaches will allow different people to more deeply understand what makes an excellent engineer, salesperson, or leader, and will also give that person a chance to coach others, which is useful as the small firm continues to grow.

 Go Beyond: Where could you try the idea of position coaches in your organization? Try it for a month and see what happens.

Lesson #8

Be Urgent in Practice, Calm in Games

Is this the worst adversity you can give us?

Boise State football player
En route to the football stadium
for the first game of the 2010 season

When Boise State's Head Football Coach, Chris Petersen, watches his players practice, he is part of the action on the field.

"Let's go, let's go. Good job, D. Good job. Come on, guys, let's pick it up."

Energy, tempo, urgency.

Petersen is adamant about the importance of energy—showing in his players when they practice, in his coaches when they lead team meetings, and in himself in each encounter he has with another person. It has a ripple effect. If coaches have poor or average energy levels, then the players will have low energy. So how does the program find out what goes on in team meetings, when coaches meet with the players within a certain position? They ask the players, every year, what could be better, including the team meetings.

When Petersen and his coaches learned that some players felt the meetings were boring, they got creative. How could they change the meetings to engage the players more, step up the energy levels, and generate more excitement? The result is partly in the way the meetings are run. Starting in the fall of 2012, the coaches and players meet twice a day for

30 minutes, rather than for one 50-minute meeting, which has been standard for several years. In the meetings, they change activities, shifting quickly from one to another. That means less time watching film, more time having players "get physical," by switching seats within the room, asking older players to help teach younger ones, and using questions more, both to engage and to see if the players are indeed learning what they need to. The pace is quick and energetic. The meetings are also videotaped, so the coaches can review their own performance to find ways to improve.

On the field, the coaches have increased the pace of practices as well. During practice, Petersen and his coaches are anything but calm. Clapping their hands, moving among the players, yelling encouragement or improvement, keeping the players moving all the time—practices are not for the laid-back, the languid, or the sluggish. And at times, the intensity affects not only the players but also others who might accidentally be nearby. The noise from the indoor practice stadium can disrupt conversation even six stories above the facility, in workshops and classes on management or finance.

"Let's go, play fast, three steps. Show us where you're going. Jog him back, jog him back, let's go, let's go." As he watches the team walk toward the end zone, kicking up their legs, Petersen says, "Let's get some elevation here. You could be a punter."

And later, "Let's see what you got, let's see it. Go! Go!"

In addition to pace, the coaches also prepare players for what will go wrong. And every time they play a game, something does. As Petersen says about so much of his job and the sport, "There's always something." It could be just a small hiccup, like meals that aren't good or hotel rooms that aren't ready on time. It could be something big, like a critical player becoming injured or a teammate who gets into trouble and will miss a game. So preparing the players for something unexpected to go wrong, and teaching them not to panic when it does, is a key aspect of building the calmness that coaches want during the game. They call it having a SWAT mentality—staying calm, no matter what.

For the first game of the 2010 football season, the Boise State team, coaches and staff members were on their way to play Virginia Tech in a stadium of nearly 90,000 (mostly Virginia Tech) fans. En route, in the midst of Washington, D.C., traffic, the first of the team's three buses broke down. The driver tried to turn over the engine. No luck. He turned to Chris Petersen.

"We'll have to call for another bus. It could take a while."

Petersen looked at the driver and then turned in his seat and faced the team.

"No way. Let's just pile into the other buses. Come on, guys, let's go."

On his way out of the door, a senior player (who went on to play in the NFL) said to the coaches, "Is this the worst adversity you can give us?"

Petersen heard later from another Boise State coach that at his former university, if a bus had broken down, it would have been a real crisis—angry coaches, upset players, and a rattled team that might have played poorly because something had gone wrong.

After what the coaches had drilled during practice, this "crisis" was nothing. The team went on to win a nail-biter game, 33-30, but did it in a state of calmness.

The intensity and sense of urgency is critical in the team meetings and in practice in large part because of what Petersen wants to happen during the game. Once the game starts, calmness prevails. Players have a sense that the pace "slows down." Because they've moved so fast and been so intense during the practices, the "real life" of the game feels slower, more easily managed and played.

Petersen models that sense of calmness and slows down himself. He doesn't yell and hardly talks or shows emotion on the sidelines. He paces the full length of the field, with a walk that the players tease him about: the short gait, quickstep, leading with his head. When he stops, he may be far away from other coaches or players. Other times, he can be hard to notice in the thick of the players and coaches because he stands so still, arms crossed, eyes hidden under his blue cap with the orange "B" on it.

Partly because of his composure, the feeling among coaches and players is cool and calm, perhaps not serene, but certainly not agitated. No screaming, no flailing arms, and no stomping back from the field when something goes wrong. The most emotion he shows may be when he leans his head back and says, "Oh, no." Then, immediately, he's back and focused, clapping, encouraging, sounding like he's in practice: "Let's go, let's go. Come on, guys, let's pick it up."

How Do Other Organizations Use It?

That mix of "urgency and calmness" plays out with other Gang organizations. Bob Lokken, CEO of WhiteCloud Analytics, incorporates the notion of urgency, especially into sales presentation practice. The salespeople repeat and repeat their presentations until they become adept and comfortable enough to deal with something going wrong and then being able to improvise. Similar to Chris Petersen, Lokken urges them to maintain a fast pace in their presentation practices so that "in real life, during a presentation, everything will seem to be in slow motion."

Law enforcement is, of course, one of the granddaddies of the idea of urgent practice and then slowing things down in a crisis situation. In many cases, it also involves becoming a team in the process. Ada County's head of detectives and SWAT teams, Pat Schneider, says that intense training matched with the right team, is critical when a crisis comes up. The physical exam to join the team is grueling. Then, the team has to accept a new member. The group trains two days per month, six hours per day, and that forms a tighter team, which, of course, pays off when they have a job to do.

In a crisis mode of a lesser kind, but one that instills a sense of high energy and urgency, Drake Cooper uses a 90-day cycle to push hard on certain tasks and ideas, and then slows down to review and reflect on what works and what does not. It's a form of mental urgency and calmness—similar to the physical ones that athletes and law enforcement officers use.

Go Beyond: In your organization, where do you use urgency and calmness?

6

Lessons From the Stage

Lesson #9

Practice to Improvise

Once you've got the fundamentals down, THEN you can get creative.

Former Boise State football offensive line player

Once [dancers] actually have a choreography that they've learned, they...perform it several times and it can't be the same performance every time. It has to be authentic to that day, to that performer and that individual.

Trey McIntyre
Choreographer

On the football field and on the stage, things go wrong. A missed pass, an interception, a missed kick—such events are the normal and expected mistakes in a game. A forgotten line, a "costume malfunction," rainfall or wildlife in an outdoor theater are the expected mistakes in a stage performance. Yet, as fans and audience members know, the show must go on, and sometimes the players, actors, and dancers just...improvise. So how do players, actors, and dancers do it?

Actors in a regional theater, such as the Idaho Shakespeare Festival, know what parts they will have in a specific play about six months before the production opens. On their own, they learn lines, research the character and play, and generally prepare long before they come to the official rehearsals, which begin about six weeks before a play opens. This is their equivalent of "the fundamentals" that football players learn when they understand the technical parts of their positions, the game, and its flow. When rehearsals start, the actors, designers, and technicians converge, and the number of people involved in the production explodes, from a small team of director and designers to the full complement of perhaps 60 people.

The director and actors rehearse often six to seven hours per day, six days a week, reviewing and experimenting with how the actors will speak, inflect, emphasize words, and move within specifics scenes. The actors repeat the scenes with one another, in front of the director, and in a whole group. Depending upon the actor and the difficulty of the part, the repetitions could run to the tens or sometimes hundreds of times. The week before the play opens is "tech week," a beta test or walk-through of the entire production. Everyone involved in the technical production of the play— from the director and designers to the technicians and actors—work together every night, for five or six days. This is the time to make sure that all the pieces work well together. Actors wear costumes and use the props, the lighting and sound/music enters, and scene shifts happen just as they will during the run of the play.

For a dance company like Trey McIntyre Project, the process is somewhat similar except that, instead of receiving already existing lines for a role, the choreographer shapes the "lines" or movements with the dancers themselves. He first tries to get out the "complicated fantasy in [his] mind," forcing dancers to take in information about where to put their arms, how to lean, and what image to think about while they are doing the moves. He might spend two hours to create 20 or 30 seconds of dance steps and movement, "revising and redrafting," just as a writer will do. Once McIntyre has gotten his ideas out and worked through multiple "drafts" with each dancer, he expects the dancer to make the movements his or her own, and then show them during the rehearsal process so they can be edited before appearing on the stage. As he says, "Part of their job is to go home at night and think through all that information and make some sense out of it for themselves for the next day moving forward." Even as the piece is being shaped, dancers continue with daily six-hour classes in technique—drills and exercises, lifting (for men), and concentrated, deliberate rehearsal.

Similarly, in football, repeated practicing of specific plays is also deliberate. The coaches may run players through a complex play six to seven times or two to three times for a simple one. The intent is the same: to execute—without mistakes—a scene in a play, a dance on stage, or a play on a field. But when things do go wrong, in each case the deliberate and concentrated repetitions and practice pays off. That's when actors, dancers, and players adjust and improvise. They have practiced to the point where they can deal with unexpected problems, have alternative options to use, and, if the coaches and directors and choreographers have done their jobs, remain unfazed and poised.

What Other Organizations Do

It's possible to imagine Jim Giuffré, Chief Operating Officer at Healthwise, as a dancer: He's lean and strong, has the grace of a long-time athlete, and is an accomplished cross-country skier, Karate black belt and mountain biker. He's an energy-saving machine: minimal body fat and few extraneous moves even in the office.

Giuffré may not be able to imagine himself as a dancer, but he has admitted that he wouldn't mind thinking like one, especially in the way that dancers practice so they can be spontaneous. The level of professionalism and quality of practice to execute a perfect play, scene, or dance, on the field or stage, astounded Giuffré when he first heard the coaches, dancers, and actors talk about it. But more interesting to him was what they are able to do when something goes wrong—they improvise.

Giuffré began wondering how "practice to improvise" might apply in a business organization. What does Healthwise do on a routine basis that could be practiced like the artists and athletes do? So many organizations, especially those that depend upon a knowledge base, seem to have activities and tasks that are nonrepetitive and thus not good candidates for "practice."

But the Healthwise executive looked harder to find areas that could use more "practice." An obvious one was client meetings. Too often, his employees go to a client meeting with a prepared presentation or plan of discussion. But then, something goes wrong: the client reduces the amount of time available, changes topics midway through the presentation, or dominates the discussion with questions and eschews the idea of a presentation altogether. If Healthwise salespeople are unable to improvise when the meeting direction shifts, it could mean loss of a potential sale or renewal.

So Giuffré applied what he had heard from actors, and dancers and coaches to develop ways for salespeople to "practice" enough that they got beyond the fundamentals, could adjust and improvise, and do what McIntyre asks his dancers to do: realize that a presentation (or "performance") can't be the same each time. As McIntyre says, "It has to be authentic to that day, to that performer and that individual," and in Healthwise's case, to that client.

Go Beyond: What areas of your organization could apply "practice to improvise"?

Lesson #10

Build Unexpected Partnerships

If we are together nothing is impossible. If we are divided all will fail.

Winston Churchill (1874-1965)
Politician and writer

Charlie Fee, Producing Artistic Director for the Idaho Shakespeare Festival, has the look you would expect from someone who's a business whiz in the arts world. Woven leather European style closed-toe sandals, khaki-colored gabardine trousers, dark, long-sleeved polo shirts: Fee does not exude the Idaho cowboy look that many try and few pull off. And he never wears a baseball cap. But he certainly knows his Shakespeare and he knows his finance.

Fee joined the Shakespeare Theater in 1991, molding it into a viable and increasingly prosperous outdoor theater. He claims that, when he realized that many of his peers were better actors than he might ever be, he switched to directing so he could still work with (meaning "hire") his acting friends. His reputation as a director has always been strong, but what set him apart was his ability to manage and keep his nonprofit organization consistently in the black. One example was his spearheading of the campaign to build a new state of the art amphitheater, fashioned in size and feel after the famed Globe Theater in Stratford, raising all of the money before beginning the construction. By the close of the 1990s, the Idaho Festival was strong financially and artistically stable, with a new outdoor facility, a highly competent administrative staff, and a strong donor base. Then Fee, the entrepreneur, got restless.

In 2002, Fee received an offer to become the artistic director of the Great Lakes Theater in Cleveland, Ohio, two thousand miles away. Initially, the intent was for him to help merge the Cleveland group with a more financially viable one. The merger collapsed, but Fee's connection to the Cleveland theater did not. He began to divide his time and efforts between Boise and Cleveland, running both theaters. While the Idaho Shakespeare Festival organization was in good shape, the Great Lakes theater was not, and Fee's job shifted from planning a merger to managing a turnaround.

Charlie Fee was raised by a finance professor father. Although he majored in theater, Fee must have absorbed a lot of dinner-table conversation about business. His first step in Cleveland was cutting costs. Once the theater was on firmer ground, he got creative and came up with an unusual partnership, unique in the regional theater world: an alliance between both theaters. Although they offer similar productions (i.e., Shakespeare plays, musicals, and one or two other classical plays per season), their seasons are complementary (Idaho's runs June—September, and Ohio's is September—May), and because they are two thousand miles apart, they do not compete.

In addition, each had organizational strengths and weaknesses that the other could learn from or help to improve. So Fee had each develop and mount two plays and then transfer them to the other theater. This allows for economies of scale, savings, and long-term loyalty of directors, actors, and designers. Bottom line: each theater gets four productions for a little more than the cost of two.

The partnership also allows Fee to hire high-quality directors, designers, and actors for longer seasons, providing them the chance for health benefits, which is uncommon in much of the performing arts world. The partnership has worked so well that Fee has begun another, in Lake Tahoe, Nevada.

Using Partners to Leverage Reach

Another Gang organization uses many types of partners to reach more customers. Healthwise's mission is to help people make better health decisions, and initially, it partnered with insurance firms that could push the health information on to clients.

Next, Healthwise pushed more information through partnering with key websites providing medical information. WebMD, for instance, which ranks as the top U.S. health care website, connects three million people per month with Healthwise information and tools.

Now, Healthwise wants to reach physicians who could advise their patients with information that will help them make good health decisions. Reaching 800,000 medical doctors in the U.S. is untenable, but a key change makes it possible for Healthwise to reach more doctors: The growth in electronic medical records (EMR) is exponential and yet the number of firms in the industry is relatively small. So by partnering with eight of the key EMR companies, Healthwise gets its information to doctors and they, in turn, can prescribe it to their patients. New partners, big gains.

Go Beyond: Do you have the best partners for what you want to do next?

Lesson #11

Create New Business Models

Imagine an alternative universe where dancers are treated like celebrities: recognized in public, lavished with gifts, fawned over by fans. They even have cocktails named after them. Now get out your atlas and locate Boise, Idaho, where the skies never seem to cloud over, the people are disconcertingly friendly, and Trey McIntyre Project is the toast of the town.

Claudia La Rocco
The New York Times, August 13, 2010

Trey McIntyre Project turned what many in the arts world considered a disadvantage into an advantage when it settled in an isolated outpost in the intermountain western U.S., far from what many people consider the creative world. A *New York Times* reporter visited the company shortly after it moved to Idaho just to see what the fuss was all about. Then she visited two years later to see what had happened. Claudia La Rocco was astounded to find that the city and company were more joined together than she could imagine.

By moving to the edge of the creative world, the group generated a different type of "buzz," and turned some disadvantages into advantages. In the process, it is helping an industry question and reinvent itself. The company moved to a place without a large financial support base, away from ready and steady "raw material sources" of dancers or designers and far from a built-in dance audience. That raises questions about just what is necessary to build a world-class, high-performing and highly creative organization. But the move was a long one in the making.

For several years, choreographer Trey McIntyre worked as resident choreographer in ballet companies, including Houston and Washington, D.C., and as a freelance choreographer for 18 years, creating dozens of commissioned works for ballet companies around the world. For three years, he ran a summer touring group, with support from donors all over the country, grant money from one of Silicon Valley's largest foundations, and performances in several top dance venues, including Jacob's Pillow in the Berkshires of Massachusetts. But when it came time to start a full-time dance company, in the middle of the 2007—2008 recession no less, he followed a strategy that was the opposite of what most people would expect. He established the company in an "unlikely" site, according to *The New York Times,* far off the beaten dance path.

McIntyre and Executive Director John Michael Schert, explored 25, then 10, cities in the United States as possible locations for their company. Settling on Boise, Idaho, far from the usual centers of dance and culture, mystified others in the creative performing arts world. To move from San Francisco, the fledgling startup dance company had to forego a one million dollar grant opportunity, which alone was a shock to other arts organizations and the granting agency. The move seemed to place the new company far from major sources of money, far from a ready supply of dancers, far from a large audience, and far from the "usual" creative stimulation.

But considering the company's philosophy, the move to an isolated outpost made perfect sense. McIntyre and Schert saw advantages where others saw disadvantages. First, TMP's board of directors and donor base come from far outside the local community, meaning the company is not location-dependent for funding. Second, rather than being hurt by being far from a trained supply of dancers, McIntyre sees it as an advantage. He recruits dancers from schools like Julliard in New York or from ballet companies in San

Francisco or Houston, and they come to Idaho (yes, Idaho) because they want to be part of *his* full-time company. Dancers in New York or San Francisco or Houston tend to be less apt to commit long term to a company, moving every year or so for more pay or better positions. Instead, by being part of a full-time company, the TMP dancers are committed not only to the choreographer and to each other but also to the community. With no other world-renowned options in town, they want to make this work. An added unexpected benefit is that they have become local "celebrities," unlikely in a large city swarming with actors, dancers, and artists.

Next, despite the lack of a ready-made audience, used to and expecting terrific cultural opportunities, this entrepreneurial start-up saw the chance to help shape an emerging arts community and build an audience rather than expect it to be there. Indeed, the performances consistently fill a 2000-person concert hall, once for the afternoon matinee and again in the evening. The feeling is like being at a rock concert, filled with people who claim they have never attended such a cultural event before in their lives. Finally, the creative stimulation that a large city offers is the antithesis of what this choreographer needs. Coming from a small town in Kansas, McIntyre is more inspired by isolation, space, and silence, and ready access to nature. Instead of "missing" the creative stimulation of a large city, McIntyre sees what others may "miss" and takes advantage of the remoteness. Since the group travels more than half the year both in the U.S. and abroad, he gets all the "external" stimulation he needs but has a quiet place to return to.

Isolation as an Advantage

Other Gang members agree that remoteness, isolation, and the shock value of being based in a place many people confuse with Iowa or Ohio has other advantages as well.

Bob Lokken, CEO of WhiteCloud, the start-up business-intelligence analytics firm, comments that turnover in an intellectual-property-based software firm is always a concern, especially in locations where competitors are nearby. By choosing to remain in a remote setting, Lokken is able to build a tight team culture of loyalty and, to some degree, an "underdog mindset," where others may not take the firm seriously…to their peril, he adds! As others have done, he uses the perceived constraint of remoteness to his firm's advantage.

Indeed, living and working in a place more known for potatoes than dance or software puts Gang members in a position of having a chip on their respective shoulders. As one leader says, "It keeps us honest, we can never believe that we're 'that' good if we come from a place that few people know of let alone care about." And even more useful, they can hide and then burst onto the competitive scene, using surprise when they come up against their, most often, much bigger and more powerful rivals. Of course, as they do gain notoriety (e.g., the Boise State football program's higher rankings), that element of surprise may fizzle.

Go Beyond: Is your business model as creative as it could be?

7

Lessons From the Boardroom

Lesson #12 Look Around the Corner

Lesson #13 Use 90-day Cycles

Lesson #14 Avoid Idea Central

Lesson #15 Change to Invigorate

Lesson #12

Look Around the Corner

My job is to look around the corner to see what's coming or what might be possible in our industry.

Don Kemper
CEO, Healthwise

If they weren't engineers, Bob Lokken and Don Kemper might be accused of having supernatural powers. They see things other people don't and look around corners to create or find opportunities and ideas where most people see mush. Their powers come, of course, in part because of logic. They place themselves strategically at corners or intersections where trends or ideas from different fields might appear. By doing that, they can see in two or more directions and in the process find connections among ideas that would be impossible to see standing just on one side of a building. Their approach supports a study of Stanford University entrepreneurs that found the entrepreneurs who were involved with people from different fields and worlds were more likely to come up with new and better business ideas. Bottom line: people who stand at intersections or at corners can see more opportunities.

Find Corners to Look Around

Before he started his latest entrepreneurial venture, Bob Lokken looked for corners that were interesting and needed to be "looked around." Instead of hoping an opportunity would just appear, Lokken systematically sought ideas that might hold promise for a future venture. He began investigating problem areas that he thought needed serious attention in the U.S. and beyond and that could use his technical business-intelligence analytics expertise of analyzing and shaping huge batches of data so people can make better decisions. After looking into education and energy, which certainly need attention, he found another one that could use his help, even if sometimes its leaders are not sure how to do it: making health care better and more efficient.

During his investigation, Lokken attended a conference for hospital CEOs. Several presenters discussed how hospitals were facing a fixed reimbursement model: The government will reimburse a certain amount for a specific operation, regardless of the hospital's costs to conduct the operation. If a hospital does the operation for less than the fixed reimbursement, it keeps the surplus profit. If a hospital spends more than the fixed reimbursement, it must cover the difference.

Then Lokken looked further around the corner to realize this meant hospitals were moving from a "price-setter model to a price-taker model, demanding efficiency" and that most hospital leaders were baffled about what to do next. On top of this, as reform looms on the horizon, it flips the hospital leaders' world upside-down, and, as Lokken says, "turns everything that is today a profit-center into a cost-center in the future."

One reason those health care leaders are in such trouble is that they lack reliable insights and understanding that could help their practices be more cost-effective. Simultaneously, in the fast-paced industry, they will be drowning in data. And that was the opportunity that Lokken saw—blending a need and his expertise. His software will allow hospitals to gather and organize massive data and make it visually accessible so physicians and administrators can make better decisions.

What Lokken saw around the corner or into the future was a way to collect and spread best-practice information to hospital managers and doctors so they could use it, and ultimately change behaviors of patients, doctors, and administrators. The challenge is not getting to the data; the challenge is how to harness the complexity and enormity of the data to generate outcomes for their patients.

See Beyond the Next Ridge

While Lokken looked around a corner for a five-year-out opportunity, others look further. Healthwise's CEO, Don Kemper, has an uncanny ability to think and see over the next ridge—10 to 20 years in his industry's future. This frustrates and fascinates people in his organization and in his industry. Kemper's future thinking started over 40 years ago when, as a young engineer and recent public administration graduate, he heard a speech that made him realize the power of patients' taking responsibility for their own health. That epiphany led Kemper, in 1975, to found Healthwise, a nonprofit health-information provider that leads the industry in "helping people make better health decisions" by providing information in accessible formats. As the organization grew, Kemper continued to look around the corner and beyond the next ridge to generate ideas that drive not only Healthwise's future but also the health care information industry generally. Seeing far ahead also helps Healthwise avoid complacency.

One example of Kemper's long-term vision was "Information Therapy" (Ix), which is "prescription information," discussed earlier. Patients are used to receiving prescriptions from their doctors for medication and Kemper imagined the same idea could be adapted for information. The notion is that a physician would write a prescription for information that a patient would use at specific times, for specific stages of a disease or purposes. From being an idea seed in the 1990s, Information Therapy (Ix) has become increasingly accepted in the health care information industry. In fact, the concept is now built into the federal government's "meaningful use" requirements for electronic medical records. All this happened because someone was able to look around a corner.

Looking Around Other Corners

Lokken's and Kemper's visionary abilities to see—and then shape—future directions for their organizations and their industries allow them to more fully plan the future of their respective organizations. In addition, if they identify new areas for expansion or ways to improve, they help their organizations avoid complacency. And interestingly, while this idea of looking into the future is common practice and "normal" in the business world, it is much less common in other fields, like football.

When Chris Petersen heard Don Kemper talking about "looking around the corner," he sat back, very intrigued at the thought, and wondered how to apply it in his field. "Don (Kemper) spends a lot of time looking around the corner, into the future. And that made me think about how I'm normally just doing what needs to get done for now—so how can I be proactive and 'look around the corner'? Think about the future?"

Instead of thinking only about an upcoming season, Petersen has begun to question where the industry of football might go, how to get ahead of the challenges facing all universities in recruiting players, and how to continue to find new ways to learn from and use ideas from outside of the sports world.

Go Beyond: How do you build future thinking into your routine, other than a programmed "strategic planning meeting?"

Lesson #13

Use 90-Day Cycles

Nothing great was ever achieved without enthusiasm.
Ralph Waldo Emerson (1803-1882)
Essayist, lecturer, and poet

Some industries have "natural cycles," allowing time for gearing up, being "on," winding down, and reflection. In theater, the director and designers work to create the production, the actors rehearse, and then the performance season begins and plays run, often six nights a week, for a set period. During the off-season, no performances happen. Likewise, university football has seasons: The primary season is during the fall semester, when games occur. The deep off-season in winter is a time to review and renew, and the off-season in late spring and summer are times to build up and try new ideas. In each case—theater or sports—the cycles or seasons allow for review and rejuvenation, to improve the upcoming season. Not so for advertising or software or law enforcement. Instead, such industries and their leaders talk about being "always on," with little time or energy to rebuild, reorganize, reflect, and celebrate.

Drake Cooper's CEO, Jamie Cooper, hails from northwestern Arkansas, Wal-Mart country, but you'd never guess it. He's "Seattle hip" but lives in Boise, Idaho. With longer-than-average "business CEO" hair, funky square glasses, and a penchant for riding his scooter or bike to work, Cooper exemplifies the marketing/advertising ethos. But he's also a tough-minded business leader, who looks for ways to improve his organization even as it deals with a chaotic industry that lacks any semblance of "natural cycles."

One way is to fail fast, often, and hard, to learn and succeed faster, more often, and better than his competitors. And he makes it happen every 90 days.

For Drake Cooper and the advertising industry in general, change, chaos and unpredictability are the normal state. As Cooper says, "In July, I have no idea what September will look like for us, in terms of business. We could be busy or everything could just fade away." That ambiguity makes it hard for some employees, who he admits probably will not last in the industry. But Cooper fears that the chaos and constant change could affect the quality of his agency's work, that it could suffer if he and his employees failed to find ways to review, rejuvenate, and reorganize on a regular basis. With no "natural cycle" that allowed for reflection and time to find ways to improve, they had to invent it.

So, Drake Cooper created its "90-day cycle," as a way to increase its agility and nimbleness but more importantly as a way to change fast. Loosely based upon the idea of agile development in software development, in which programmers work intensely for short "sprints," review work, fix problems, and move forward. At the start of each of Drake Cooper's 90-day cycles, leaders set goals and ideas for the organization and employees pursue and try them out. In addition, employees match up in pairs, often not from the same area, to act as mentors or "idea bouncers" for each other. This allows them to get to know others around the firm, to test ideas fast, and to learn from and coach each other.

The outcome is to determine what to "stop, start, and continue." The cycle encourages a "hard push" sprint for 90 days, during which the team tries a few specific ideas. At the close of the 90 days, Cooper says, "The shop comes together, reviews successes, cries over failures, talks out issues, and looks at how to adopt things that are working and nix those that are not." In the process, the group learns to "fail fast to learn faster."

Other Cycles

Other Gang members have built in cycles of different periods while some have not. Healthwise uses agile development in its "sprints" to develop software but has begun to apply the notion of fast cycles in other parts of the organization. Leaders do stop to assess on a regular basis—quarterly, during annual planning, and every three years during strategic planning.

The Ada County Sheriff's Office is one of The Gang members that, like Drake Cooper, is in a constant mode of change and unpredictability, given the nature of its "industry." Yet, when Gary Raney heard about Cooper's 90-day cycle idea, he was intrigued. Since he tends to focus on the future, always "looking forward," Raney says he is less inclined to stop and reflect and review what seems to be working. Yet, he's considering starting a similar type of program—maybe not 90 days but 120 or 180 days. The agency might identify some new tactics to try, check, adjust, and try again.

Go Beyond: How do you get employees to reflect, learn from each other, and stay charged on a regular basis?

Lesson #14

Avoid Idea Central

Everyone is a genius at least once a year. The real geniuses simply have their bright ideas closer together.

Georg Christoph Lichtenberg (1742-1799)

German physicist

Healthwise founder Don Kemper has a craggy face, a head of bushy white hair, and a large wide smile. Although he seems laid back and mellow, he could never be accused of being retiring when it comes to the way he thinks and talks about ideas. His ideas come fast and close together, they are diverse, and to people unfamiliar with his style, he can be intimidating because of the quantity and wide-ranging ferocity of those ideas. His employees say that Kemper can be five to ten years ahead of his organization, let alone his industry. So it's a safe bet that some of his ideas might even outlive him. But, even now, can any organization afford to depend upon one or a few people for ideas? How can more people become "idea geniuses" and have ideas closer together, as Georg Lichtenberg suggested so many years ago?

Kemper's situation is not unusual for people like The Gang leaders, who are always seeking ways to out think, out innovate, and out perform their peers. They want to avoid complacency, look around corners, see what others miss, and get better every day. And because of the force of their personalities, in some cases, the leaders become what one Gang member called "Idea Central," the wellspring of some of the best ideas that the organization may pursue. That can be good…and bad.

Having leaders who are relentless about learning and getting better and finding ways to keep their organizations ahead of any peers is, of course, enviable. As the quote at the chapter's beginning suggests, some people are good at having ideas come closer together and more often, which is something most Gang leaders can do. Yet, relying too much on one or a few people for new ideas and directions is loaded with danger, for at least four reasons.

First, environments—whether technologies, customers or competitors—change, and to be ahead of those changes, ideas must also change. And while some leaders may be able to generate new ideas that lead or shape an industry and organization, no one person can or should do it all. So finding ways to encourage and nourish the innovative ideas of more people is critical to any organization's future.

Second, relying on just a few people in an organization to generate ideas limits the organization dramatically, simply because the number of good ideas would be greater with more brainpower. Bob Lokken and other leaders at his former firm, ProClarity, recognized early that they needed to expand the number of "touch points" the firm had with the external environment. Touch points referred to the chances that someone in the organization could talk to customers, competitors, suppliers, and other professionals. Since Lokken and the other senior leaders could only do so much, the number of contacts or touch points, and likely information and ideas coming from them, could increase if more people in ProClarity were involved. Thus, they encouraged people from all levels to generate touch points, making more contacts externally, and boosting the firm's reach and ability to see trends, find new ideas, and connect dots that the leaders might not see.

Third, and perhaps most frightening for organizations fearful of complacency, is the risk that depending on Idea

Central will lead to complacency in others. As is true for many members of the The Gang, their leaders generate good ideas daily, weekly, and yearly. Because they tend to be such idea machines, it could be easy for others to refrain from jumping into the idea fray. But if people rely on and expect others (or a few) to generate ideas, then they lose the skill of coming up with new ideas. As Sheriff Gary Raney says, once employees start to "delegate up," they lose the ability to do a task themselves, like generating new ideas. Coming up with new ways of doing some task is hard work. Without learning how to do it and practicing it deliberately, that skill atrophies.

And last, if encouraged, the Idea Central people might themselves become complacent. If they start to assume that their ideas are good enough to carry the organization forward, they will likely fail. Since members of The Gang desperately fear becoming complacent, the leaders keep reminding themselves to continue to push for high output in ideas and to keep their egos in check.

The solution: Gang leaders are conscientiously building in the notion of "ideas from all levels." Healthwise includes "relentless innovation" as one of its core competencies. Coach Chris Petersen and Sheriff Gary Raney frequently ask their employees to find new ways to achieve a goal. And Trey McIntyre, simply by creating new dances each year, models the idea of doing things differently, not just in the art but also throughout the organization.

Go Beyond: How can you get more ideas from people who don't think they have any to offer?

Lesson #15

Change to Invigorate

We try to change something on a regular basis. The players adapt to it and…then over time, they even expect change.
Tim Socha
Strength Training Coach, Boise State University

Bob Lokken, the software CEO, long ago looked to the film industry for ideas about software design but also for ways to organize teams. Film productions assemble experts from different fields (e.g., actors, tech people, costumers, and directors) for a project that ideally is completed on time, on budget, and with high quality. Then the experts shift to new projects, invigorated and energized.

Trying to keep the energy in his organization high, Lokken and other senior leaders modified the film team idea to develop a bidding process for software projects, which shuffled people and managers from project to project. Engineers requested to be on certain projects or to work with specific managers. Managers could, in turn, invite specific people for their projects and the engineers could decide whom they wanted to work for.

The result: the bidding process encouraged both engineers and managers to be top-notch so they would be selected. Engineers had to stay up in their fields technically but also be good team members, and managers needed to have interesting projects and be good to work for. In the process, the teams remained energetic, and each project change helped invigorate the individuals.

Several Gang organizations have found that, in addition to causing heartburn because change is uncomfortable, it can also invigorate. Several of them have systematically built change into their operations, and sometimes found some unexpected outcomes.

Lift Sandbags, Not Barbells

When football players start practice in the summer, the schedule is clear, planned long in advance, and has a rhythm to it that the students learn, accept, and expect. They know that running comes before lifting and that the weight room is for lifting. But what happens when they arrive one day and the schedule is reversed? What happens if they do lifts outside, instead of in the weight room, and what if they have to use sandbags, not barbells?

Strength Training Coach Tim Socha smiles when he talks about the looks on the surprised, sometimes annoyed, players' faces when they first hear him bark out the changes for the day. And then he smiles even bigger when he thinks about what happens over time: The players get used to change, expect it, and become more energized. It keeps the training fresh and invigorating.

Jail to Patrol to Jail to Patrol

Within law enforcement, an inherent divide seems to exist between the areas of patrol and the jail. The duties are very different and the interaction between groups is limited. As a result, little understanding exists across different jobs.

Sgt. Pat Calley, having worked in both areas, put it this way:

> The patrol guys have *no* idea of the workload each day when they start. The stress level can go up and down dramatically within that day. The jail guys have the same work load every day, all day and it's high stress. They must be

vigilant in the dorms all day long without a break.

In many agencies, managers see the divide between the two areas as just the nature of the organization. Not so at the Ada County Sheriff's Office. The sheriff and his senior managers want a culture of one single organization with several different functions, each dependent upon the others. To that end, people in supervision and management often transfer to assignments in different areas, often to functions unfamiliar to them.

Transferring people across areas accomplishes three goals, both for the employees and for the organization. First, as people learn the different areas during their career, they understand better the interaction and impact of one area on others. For instance, a new requirement during the jail intake procedure might cause a significant delay for the patrol deputies, keeping them from returning to patrol duty.

When people in one area worry about their own interests without taking into account the impact on other areas, bureaucracy develops. But when members in all areas share the same goals and understanding of what really matters, it's possible to reduce bureaucracy.

A second benefit of transfers is that the new person assigned to an area almost always brings fresh perspectives and questions. The Sheriff's Office encourages these "new" people to ask questions like "Why do we do that?" But more than just asking, they should refuse to accept the pat answer, "Because that's the way we've always done it."

These new perspectives and ideas have led to many changes that have transformed—and improved—the agency. The shifting across functional areas is integral and critical to the agency's being a learning organization.

Last, by shifting employees between the areas, individuals build respect and understanding for the other units, and they begin to see the bigger picture—how the whole organization works and how units within it (should) work together.

Go Beyond: What can you do to help people use change and see it as a good thing?

Start Your Own Gang

Why and How?

You've learned about The Gang from Boise, and maybe you want to start your own gang. As we've talked about The Gang regionally, nationally and even internationally, we've had a lot of requests to join or start a gang. As a result, we've started five other groups in the last few years to see if we could replicate the idea. The Posse, The Hard Rock Miners, The Wranglers, and The Sidewinders (we do live in the Wild West, after all) have succeeded. A fifth group fizzled, but we learned from the experience. Each has a different type of membership, but the core features remain the same.

The lessons we've learned and continue to learn on how to form and facilitate new gangs might help if you are interested in forming one. So in this last chapter, we first describe the benefits of a gang to help you decide whether it makes sense to form one of your own. Then, we'll give you tips from what we've learned that can help increase the chance of your gang's success.

Benefits of a Gang

The Gang in Boise has been in place for over six years. It's taken time for the members to get to know one another and to move past using the professor in the group as a "switch board" where she hears ideas from one Gang member and mentions them to another. Now Gang leaders go directly to each other with questions and ideas. The group meets once a year with employees from each organization, but a smaller group meets irregularly (about bi-monthly) and has morphed in its purpose over the years to focus more on how this group of smart people might make changes in the community, not just within their own organizations. Because the leaders of The Gang are busy, it's hard for them to block regular time to meet, yet they continue to find it valuable when they can.

What do Gang members gain then, from being part of such a group? Over the years, leaders and members report several benefits, but three stand out. First, Gang leaders value the ideas, views, and wisdom that come from *organizations that are beyond their fields and disciplines.* This book is evidence of the many commonalities Gang members share as well as some of the ideas they've adopted from each other. That the ideas come from the arts, business, government, and sports/education shows the power of the diversity.

Second, Gang members offer *nonjudgmental sounding boards* for each other. Leaders at the tops of organizations can be lonely. They may find it difficult to get ideas that might push them in new ways. Because The Gang organizations are not in the same sectors, they do not compete, which allows for open discussion. Also, no one has a direct stake in whether ideas are used or tossed, so egos do not come into play.

Finally, at one meeting, each Gang leader realized how interconnected their organizations and goals are: *they all want a stronger economic region.* The coach cannot recruit students unless the city is safe (the sheriff's job) and unless employment is strong (the CEOs' jobs); the CEOs and the sheriff can't recruit employees without quality cultural and sports events (dance, theater, football) or educational opportunities (the university). Thus, as they come to know each other, they can work even more closely to build the components of the region and its economy. The benefits, then, range from personal development and growth to boosting organizational performance with new ideas to building a stronger community.

Start Your Own Gang

What are the critical factors in creating and facilitating a gang of aggressive learners?

We start with a few critical fundamentals. First, gang members must be *aggressive learners, relentlessly curious, and high-output, low ego people*. This means being willing to listen, learn, and do. Without these qualities, the group is a non-starter.

Second, gang members must represent *wildly different fields* and thus come from *noncompeting organizations*. The Posse includes some younger people from younger organizations, ranging from hospitality to youth sports, the arts, and business. The Hard Rock Miners, The Wranglers and The Sidewinders tend to be somewhat more experienced and are from government, education, the law, the arts, sports, business, and even the zoo! Different backgrounds, experiences, and perspectives are the core of gang success. No diversity, no learning.

Third, one surprise that is now obvious to us but was not initially is that when *people do not know each other ahead of time*, the group coalesces faster. Why? First, each person must speak in simple English (not in their field's jargon) and they're forced to tell their stories in a fresh way. All slates are blank, and we all learn together from scratch.

Finally, when a *facilitator identifies and vets the members*, it adds credibility to the process. By having an objective outsider select and help shape the group, it also boosts expectations that each member will be someone credible to learn from. The one group that dissolved began with a single person who identified some friends he wanted to learn from. The group came from different fields, to be sure, but the members never all quite had the commitment to the group and to a common goal: learning. Also, because some members knew each other (well), there were threads of connections that not everyone knew or followed. That is not necessarily bad, but it changed the nature of the group.

In addition to being involved in forming the group, a *facilitator can help pose questions, move discussions along, and bring new knowledge* to the discussion as well. Further, a facilitator can be the "nudger" to call meetings and corral very busy participants. In that vein, we've found that having a set date, time, and place to meet and sticking to it, helps continuity. Not everyone will join every session, but even if a couple of people meet, the discussion and learning can continue.

So there you go. The secrets of forming a gang: find aggressive learners, recruit people from diverse fields whom you don't know, and have someone help facilitate.

Now get moving. We'd like to see cities and states and countries everywhere form gangs of aggressive learners.

Summary Of
Rules and Lessons

Rules

Rule #1 **Look Beyond Your Field**—Use ideas from disciplines other than your own.

Rule #2 **Blend Structure and Creativity**—Use routine and structure as the core for creativity.

Rule #3 **Make Aha! Moments Happen**—Make creativity a habit.

Rule #4 **Fear Complacency**—Always ask, "How can we do this differently and better?"

Rule #5 **Turn Disadvantages into Advantages**—Look in directions your competitors do not.

Rule #6 **Change Your Mind, Not Your Mission**—Be open to changing but certain of the goals.

Rule #7 **Think BIG**—Just because you're small, don't let that limit you.

Rule #8 **Build a Culture of Performance**—Get the right people, have the right goals, and be transparent.

Rule #9 **Ask, Don't Tell**—Use questions to understand, engage, solve and find problems.

Rule #10 **Time Your Big Moves**—Listen to yourself and then test it.

Rule #11 **Make the Unimagined Real**—Dream it and do it.

Lessons

Lesson #1 **Use Reverse Thinking**—Look upside down for solutions to problems.

Lesson #2 **See What's Missing**—Look for the gaps that others don't see.

Lesson #3 **Seek Ideas From All Levels**—Avoid dependence on a few people for ideas.

Lesson #4 **Build a Problem-Solving Mindset**—Focus on outcomes, not processes.

Lesson #5 **Use Whole-Part-Whole Learning**—Go from big picture to details to big picture and back.

Lesson #6 **Get Better EDD (Every Damn Day)**—Practice deliberately.

Lesson #7 **Develop Position Coaches**—Build experts and let them teach.

Lesson #8 **Be Urgent in Practice, Calm in Games**—Push hard, then slow down.

Lesson #9 **Practice to Improvise**—Get the fundamentals down and then you're ready for surprises.

Lesson #10 **Build Unexpected Partnerships**—Find unusual links and connections.

Lesson #11 **Create New Business Models**—Go where the competition isn't.

Lesson #12 **Look Around the Corner**—Think ahead no matter what your field.

Lesson #13 **Use 90-Day Cycles**—Find ways to keep the energy up.

Lesson #14 **Avoid Idea Central**—Encourage ideas from beyond your "idea machines".

Lesson #15 **Change to Invigorate**—Encourage comfort with change.

Acknowledgements

We have so many people to thank for helping bring *Wise Beyond Your Field* to life, but we'd like to thank some in particular.

Thanks to Stephanie Chism, Joanna Lui, Rebekah McGoughty, and Tia Briggs for production, Paul Carew of Carew Co. for design, Jesse Baker, and Max Corbet for marketing guidance and support, the faculty, staff, and students of Boise State University's College of Business and Economics for being guinea pigs on parts of the book, and the Executive MBA5s for feedback (irreverent, as usual) on the book cover.

Ryan Cooper (U.S. Navy, MD to be), Bianca Jochimsen (Google), and Larissa Lee (University of Utah law student) were great and helpful graduate assistants during many of the years we learned about The Gang.

Boise State University's General Counsel Office, especially Rachel Bickerton, helped through some legal lessons. Matt Wagner of Fresh Books believed in the book and sparked us to get it done.

Many others have been long supporters and advocates for The Gang. Several of them have been great editors and sounding boards, including Renee Anchustegui, Hildy Ayer, Linda Clark-Santos, Heidi Dewey, Hal Eastman, Dave Harbison, Cheryl Larabee, Matt Larabee, Tony Olbrich, Rich Raimondi, Kirk Smith, and Angeli Weller.

We are especially grateful for the support from Bob Kustra, President of Boise State University, and Pat Shannon, Dean of the College of Business and Economics at Boise State University. Both have been Gang fans for years and we appreciate it.

References

Bryant, Adam. 2011. *The Corner Office: Indispensable and Unexpected Lessons from CEOs on how to lead and succeed.* New York: Times Books.

Covey, Stephen M.R. and Merrill, R. R. 2008. *The Speed of Trust: The One Thing That Changes Everything.* New York: Free Press.

Colvin, Geoff. 2010. *Talent Is Overrated: What Really Separates World-Class Performers from Everybody Else.* New York: Portfolio Trade.

About the Authors

Nancy K. Napier, Director of the Centre for Creativity and Innovation at Boise State University and Adjunct Professor at Aalborg University (Denmark), scours the world for ideas—from Vietnam to Botswana. Mostly, she loves the ones from The Gang and its offshoots and hopes this book will inspire wise gangs to spring up everywhere.

Jamie Cooper, CEO of Drake Cooper, has helped his firm achieve many professional awards, whistles on his bike as he rides to work, and, if he ever needed a new career, could do impressions.

Mark Hofflund, Managing Director of the Idaho Shakespeare Festival, was appointed to the National Endowment of the Arts, ran track for Princeton in college, and knows how to deal with *real* stage wildlife, as in deer, geese, and skunks, as well as anyone.

Don Kemper, founder and CEO of Healthwise, is a regular national and international speaker on consumer health care issues, invites well-behaved dogs to join their owners at work, and walks more miles than most people drive.

Bob Lokken, founder and CEO of WhiteCloud Analytics, has given in to being an unrelenting serial entrepreneur who once tried to retire to play golf but decided that was harder work than starting new firms.

Chris Petersen, Head Football Coach at Boise State University, is tenacious about finding ways to improve and devilish in challenging his coaches and players to do the same, and if he ever needed a new job, he could open a library, starting with all the books in his office.

Gary Raney, Sheriff of the Ada County Sheriff's Office, once said an inmate's escape was a *good* thing—to help the office throw off complacency. His untapped talent is organizing competitive cooking events.

John Michael Schert, Executive Director and Co-founder of Trey McIntyre Project, must be one of the few international dancers who also played a mean game of football in Valdosta, Georgia, as a youngster.

Made in the USA
San Bernardino, CA
07 September 2013